IT'S 2AM AT 1600 PENNSYLVANIA AVENUE

Case Studies on Leadership

Jeffrey J. Porter

Independently published

Copyright © 2022 Jeffrey J. Porter

All rights reserved.

No part of this book may be reproduced, or stored in a retrieval system, or transmitted in any form or by any means, electronic, mechanical, photocopying, recording, or otherwise, without express written permission of the publisher. The only exception is the visual images/photographs that are in the public domain and/or credited in this book.

ISBN: 9798432083548 (paperback)
ISBN: 9798432923257 (hardcover)

US Copyright Registration: TXu002302657

Independently published in the United States of America.

Our truest life is when we are in dreams awake.

HENRY DAVID THOREAU

CONTENTS

Title Page
Copyright
Epigraph
Dedication — 1
Introduction — 2
Presidential Reflections on Leadership — 5
Case Studies — 7
Case 1: Firing a Popular Military General — 8
Case 2: Facing Down Treason — 13
Case 3: "Nothing To Fear" — 17
Case 4: Power Struggle — 21
Case 5: Going Down Fighting — 26
Case 6: Upholding The Rule Of Law — 32
Case 7: Strategic Governance — 37
Case 8: Seeking Common Ground — 41
Case 9: Act Of Justice, Part A — 46
Case 10: Act Of Justice, Part B — 51
Case 11: Camelot — 56
Case 12: "Fear No Evil" — 61
Case 13: Art Of Diplomacy — 67
Case 14: The Comeback Kid — 72
Case 15: In Reverence For The Office, Part A — 77

Case 16: In Reverence For The Office, Part B	82
Case 17: Fighting The Status Quo	86
Case 18: Eyeball To Eyeball	92
case 19: Compassion For The Broken	96
Case 20: Reassuring A Stricken Nation	102
Case 21: Battling The Subordinate	108
Case 22: Firm Hold On The Electorate	113
Test Your Knowledge	119
Answer Key	122
References	123
About The Author	128
Afterword	130

✲ ✲ ✲

DEDICATION

To Kandace, Morgan, and Mason, who have patiently listened to my impromptu stories about American presidents over the years.

✲ ✲ ✲

✼ ✼ ✼

INTRODUCTION

Leadership has never been easy, but leaders of virtually any type of organization today are faced with intense scrutiny and criticism as never before. Instead of seeking to understand the decisions by those that seek solutions to an organization's problems, many stakeholders have become more accustomed to finding fault no matter what the topic. The COVID-19 pandemic has exasperated the tensions for those who lead organizations, often with about half of the stakeholders in favor and the other half opposed to any major decision made.

It's 2 AM at 1600 Pennsylvania Avenue is a series of actual leadership challenges faced by American presidents. When wrestling with life's most vexing problems, it is human nature to lie awake in the middle of the night contemplating ways to bring resolution to those issues. The cases illustrated in this book and their accompanying reflective activities involving the decisions made by the nation's chief executives are not intended to provide answers for those who seek them, but rather a reminder that leaders at all levels are faced with intensive decision-making with common patterns and themes. Continuous reflective practice using actual case examples can help build strong skills to meet the challenges of leadership. This book blends historical cases faced by various US presidents with general applicability that can serve as a guide to anyone who wishes to study leadership and its lasting impact on people and their organizations.

Many of the noble characteristics that we associate with leadership are illustrated in this book. Abraham Lincoln practiced humility when comforting both a dying soldier and a grieving mother who had lost several children to the Civil War. Harry Truman had every reason to throw the towel in when running for reelection in 1948, but was unwavering in his belief that he could overcome the obstacles. Woodrow Wilson stuck to his ideals at great personal cost. Franklin Roosevelt provided a sense of stability and optimism in the face of two of the greatest crises in American history. And Chester Arthur shed his corrupt past and conducted the presidency with dignity and grace.

These same characteristics, and many more, can also define the leadership styles of leaders of any organization today. Instead of lying awake at 2 AM reinventing the wheel, try learning from some of American history's most notable actors as they tackled their own leadership dilemmas. You'll be surprised how many parallels your current crisis has to a once-occupant of the big home on Pennsylvania Avenue in Washington, DC. By examining the trials and perseverance of those who have occupied the White House over the last 230 years, we can harness the lessons of our nation's instructive and illustrative history to lead us forward with confidence and reassurance.

Regards,

Jeffrey J. Porter

JEFFREY J. PORTER

* * *

❋ ❋ ❋

PRESIDENTIAL REFLECTIONS ON LEADERSHIP

Nearly all men can stand adversity, but if you want to test a man's character, give him power. Abraham Lincoln

There are many ways of going forward, but only one way of standing still. Franklin D. Roosevelt

Any man worth his salt will stick up for what he believes is right, but it takes a slightly better man to acknowledge instantly and without reservation that he is in error. Andrew Jackson

Absolute identity with one's cause is the first and great condition of successful leadership. Woodrow Wilson

A leader cannot always be popular. Harry S Truman

Surround yourself with the best people you can find, delegate authority, and don't interfere as long as the policy you've decided upon is being carried out. Ronald Reagan

Leadership and learning are indispensable to each other. John F. Kennedy

Leadership to me means duty, honor, and country. It means character, and it means listening from time to time. George W. Bush

A good leader can't get too far ahead of his followers. Franklin D. Roosevelt

The best leader is the one who has sense enough to pick good men to do what he wants done, and the self-restraint to keep from meddling with them while they do it. Theodore Roosevelt

❋ ❋ ❋

✽ ✽ ✽

CASE STUDIES

American Presidents Put to the Test

* * *

CASE 1: FIRING A POPULAR MILITARY GENERAL

Harry S Truman (1945-53)

President Harry S Truman allowed the nation to become embroiled in an unpopular conflict with Korea during the early 1950s. The conflict resulted from North Korea's invasion of its southern neighbor with the full backing of the Soviet Union. Truman used the Korean invasion as an example of the need to carry out his policy of "containment" to thwart the expansion of communism. This war came just five years after World War II ended, and the American public was understandably weary of another overseas entanglement.

Despite the war's unpopularity, the commanding general of the multinational forces was a distinguished and beloved military leader in the person of Douglas MacArthur. MacArthur's charismatic personality and immense confidence and success as a military officer made him appear to be larger than life and "untouchable" in many respects. For these reasons, President Truman maintained a long-standing relationship of uneasiness with his star general, often ignoring many small matters over the years that created a rift between the two men.

Much of these tensions arose from MacArthur's resentment of the president's ascension in 1945, replacing long-time President Franklin Roosevelt, who had earned the respect and admiration of the general and the nation. In 1950, Truman traveled half way across the world to confer in person with Gen. MacArthur on Wake Island with regards to war strategy. He made this trip partly to avoid summonsing the general to Washington DC, fearing such a meeting would be distracting and provide MacArthur with a stage to further solidify his support with the American public. Upon reaching Wake Island, Truman was forced to wait 45 minutes while his subordinate delayed his own arrival. The President chastised his general for this obvious slight, yet continued amicably with their meeting in order to ensure their mutual understanding and working relationship. As Truman was leaving the island, MacArthur failed to salute the President, a customary sign of respect. This second slight did not go unnoticed, but Truman decided to ignore it.

President Truman returned to the U.S. after Wake Island thinking he and Gen. MacArthur were on the same page with regards to war strategy. He would soon discover that this was not the case. In the meantime, China had entered the conflict in support of North Korea and the Soviet Union. This new development threatened to widen the war and lead to a potential third world war. Gen. MacArthur's calls for increased troops and a naval blockade of China were immediately rejected by the President. The general was angry at this decision and announced his displeasure with this strategy to the press without Truman's knowledge or consent. Instead of formally reprimanding the general, a gag order was generically placed on all military commanders which required them to clear all press releases with the White House.

Meanwhile, President Truman had secretly begun talks with North Korea in the spring of 1951 around possible peace negotiations to end the conflict. MacArthur had knowledge of these dealings and upstaged the President's planned announcement of the peace talks by again using the press for his purposes. Deliberately baiting China in a press release, all chances of peace talks were compromised and Truman was forced to abandon his announcement to this effect. Yet, once again Truman chose to take no formal disciplinary action against his popular general. Then came another insubordinate act, this time a letter to several members of Congress criticizing the President's handling of the conflict and his policy of limited war. This letter was read publicly on the floor of the House of Representatives and was widely published.

Truman could no longer ignore the blatant insubordination and decided to relieve MacArthur of his duties. He sent the general a secure cable of his decision and made efforts to ensure that MacArthur would not be leaked the decision and resign first. Truman held an unscheduled press conference in the middle of the night to publicly announce his termination of the general. As expected, President Truman's decision created an uproar in the country and a backlash that resulted in congressional hearings and subsequent low ratings for the remainder of his term in office.

Years later, President Truman explained his decision to fire Gen. MacArthur. "I didn't fire him because he was a dumb son-of-a-__, although he was. I fired him because he wouldn't respect the authority of the President." Historians attribute Truman's action as a critical affirmation of the importance of civilian control of the military. The passions of 1951 have been replaced over time by the understanding that the Constitution must be protected and maintained by keeping the military in check. President Truman reminded the nation that civilians, not military commanders and officers, must exercise control of the government at all times despite prevailing conditions.

* * *

Truman Presidential Library

President Truman with Gen. MacArthur at Wake Island, 1950

* * *

Case 1 Reflection

1. Why did President Truman wait so long to relieve General MacArthur?

2. What benefits can result from leaders ignoring or marginalizing insubordinate behavior?

3. How does an employee's standing with others play into how a leader chooses to handle inappropriate behavior?

4. What parameters may leaders place on the 1st Amendment free speech rights of employees?

5. Would you have been as patient as President Truman given a related set of circumstances as a leader? Why or why not?

6. President Truman wanted to make sure that Gen. MacArthur did not have an opportunity to resign before his termination was officially relayed. Why do you think this was important to Truman?

7. Why are some decisions extremely unpopular at the time but are later viewed as bold and wise? What is a contemporary example of a leader who has made a controversial decision only to later be praised for the same decision?

* * *

CASE 2: FACING DOWN TREASON

Andrew Jackson (1829-37)

Andrew Jackson was swept into office in 1828 by appealing to the "Common Man" and his belief in the limitations of government in the lives of ordinary citizens. His Vice President, John C. Calhoun, was in fact an ardent States' Rights proponent to which both men found much common ground. Jackson worked to reverse many of the nationalistic policies that strengthened the central government during the first several administrations of the young nation. He successfully dissolved the Bank of the United States for fear of its stranglehold on the nation's finances. So, when the greatest crisis of Jackson's presidency erupted in 1831, many thought the President would side with the rebellious state of South Carolina. They were wrong.

When Congress passed a new tariff law that proved unfavorable to South Carolina and several other states in the South, Vice President Calhoun worked with officials in that state to oppose the new congressional law. Their defense evolved from the doctrine of nullification, whereby a state can veto a national law it disagreed with. After a bill was introduced in Congress to legitimize nullification, Sen. Daniel Webster fought back with these words: "When my eyes shall be turned to behold for the last time the sun in heaven, may I not see Him shining in the broken and dishonored fragments of a once glorious Union." Webster led the charge in Congress against any form of nullification, and Vice President Calhoun resigned his office to represent South Carolina in the Senate in order to lead the nullification faction. All were prepared for a massive showdown that could put the nation at risk of disunion.

President Jackson realized the gravity of the conflict. He also realized that if states could nullify a national law, then the very existence of the country was at risk. As a result, though he was grounded in limited central government, Jackson found himself enraged by the idea of a broken nation. He chose a bold and decisive course that included no compromising and no turning back. In December 1832, he issued a proclamation to the people of South Carolina, declaring "The laws of the United States must be executed. Disunion by armed force is treason. Are you ready to incur its guilt?" He then assured the nation in a final and unrelenting statement, "Union men, fear not. The Union will be preserved."

Jackson began mobilizing the army, threatening to call up 200,000 soldiers to march into South Carolina, an enormous investment at that time. This strong action convinced other sympathetic southern states to abandon any plans to join South Carolina in its nullification fight.Congress responded by passing a compromise tariff bill and South Carolina promptly withdrew its ordinance of nullification. What could have been a severe crisis leading to civil war was averted, at least for a while. But it settled the issue of nullification for good, never to be brought to the national forefront again.

Case 2 Reflection

1. President Jackson and Vice President Calhoun had been friends and ideological colleagues until the issue of nullification surfaced. Why is it important for the two top leaders of an organization to be of the same mindset, at least publicly, and to give the appearance of supporting each other?

2. Andrew Jackson believed in a limited national government, yet forcefully responded when this same government was threatened. How do leaders reconcile their philosophical beliefs with their required duties?

3. Leadership often involves consensus building and compromise. However, are there occasions when leaders should and must take bold and decisive action?

4. How can the words and actions of the leader influence the direction of an organization?

5. Despite his philosophical beliefs, Andrew Jackson nonetheless vastly expanded the powers of the presidency during his two terms in office. What personality and leadership qualities contributed to Jackson's broad appeal that can be translated to other organizations?

6. President Jackson was known for meaning what he said, and South Carolina knew that he would send an army to force compliance if needed. How did this important quality help to diffuse what could have been a dangerous situation? Can you think of an example where a leader used idle words that ended up contributing to a worsening situation?

JEFFREY J. PORTER

Matthew Brady

President Andrew Jackson did not suffer treason lightly

* * *

CASE 3: "NOTHING TO FEAR"

Franklin D. Roosevelt (1933-45)

It was the depth of the worst economic depression in American history. Fifteen million workers (one-quarter of the nation's workforce) were unemployed, five thousand banks had shut their doors in 38 states, millions had lost their life's savings, millions more were on the verge of losing their homes, and soup lines were commonplace in nearly every community. Capitalism, as it appeared to many people, was in danger of collapsing. It was against this bleak backdrop that Franklin D. Roosevelt took the oath of office on March 4, 1933. He knew that if he did not boldly and promptly respond to the crisis before him, he could very well be the last U.S. president in history.

Fortunately, Roosevelt (or FDR as he was affectionately referred to), met this challenge head on. Declaring that "this great nation will revive and prosper" and that "the only thing we have to fear is fear itself," FDR aggressively experimented with action-oriented programs and policies to fight the Depression. During his first 100 days in office, he pushed Congress to adopt many new governmental initiatives to secure retirement savings, put people back to work, and save the nation's farming industry. Later, he introduced further reforms that included the Social Security Act of 1935, providing for the care of elderly and unemployed citizens to further what FDR called a "New Deal" for the American people.

FDR was born into wealth, yet he connected easily with average citizens, becoming the champion of the neediest Americans within a short period of time. He used radio to communicate directly with people through frequent and highly popular "fireside chats" that allowed FDR to explain government initiatives in everyday terminology with confidence and reassurance. In fact, his ability to resonate with millions of Americans led *Fortune Magazine* to describe FDR as the "best voice in radio." This ability to marshal the courage to handle the crisis of the Great Depression transferred to World War II after the United States was unexpectedly attacked at Pearl Harbor. On December 7, 1941, thousands of sailors were killed by the Japanese in a sneak attack that destroyed eighteen warships and 177 air force planes. This attack occurred within the context of a dark world where Western Europe had already fallen to Germany. The very existence of civilization clung in the balance as FDR awoke the morning after Pearl Harbor to prepare for his speech on Capitol Hill declaring war on Japan.

FDR's preparation for the short trip to the Capitol may seem insignificant, but for him it was monumental. Since 1921, he had dealt with the severe effects of polio which had left him completely paralyzed from the waist down. Unable to move his legs or walk, he required the use of ten pounds of steel leg braces that locked at the knees when making public appearances along with a cane and an aide's assistance. Even then, walking was difficult for him, and the long center aisle down the crowded House of Representatives was almost beyond his ability to maneuver. But FDR knew he had no choice but to appear strong and unrelenting to a fearful public.

As he did on so many other occasions during his twelve years in office, President Roosevelt overcame his physical disability for the good of the nation. Enduring the hour-long ritual of aides outfitting him with leg braces and three large straps that went across his legs and hips to provide rigid support for his lifeless legs, FDR then left the White House for the short drive. But on this day, December 8, the United States was already at war. The Secret Service took extraordinary precautions that have rarely been duplicated in history for fear of an assassination attempt.

As the crippled president finally made his way to the rostrum after the painful walk down the chamber's long center aisle, his son reflected on what must have been occupying his father's mind: it was not his speech, the impending war, or the gravity of the moment. Instead, James Roosevelt knew that his father's "uppermost thought was that he get one braced foot after another in the right position; that he hold his balance just so; that he shift his shoulders forward, left, and right just so; that he not fall down." All of this was done in the glaring lights of the press's broadcast of the historic speech to the world. FDR could make no mistakes, and he did not. Once again, he roused the country with his strong voice and conviction that "this is a day that will live in infamy" and began the long journey into World War II. Just like the Depression, he would comfort and lead the nation through another crisis without fear. A reporter later reflected on FDR's significance: "You have to remember that he arrived during Depression days and remained into the war. These were hard times, and he was our hope."

Case 3 Reflection

1. President Roosevelt proved skillful in both inspiring and comforting the nation through his words and mannerisms, qualities that helped soften the impact of the Great Depression and World War II. How can organizational leaders use FDR's example?

2. FDR was masterful at crisis management, competently handling two of the most devastating events in U.S. history. What specific leadership techniques can be applied to the successful resolution of crises in other organizations?

3. How did FDR's paralysis shape him as a leader? Have you known leaders who have overcome disabilities and used this as a strength in their leadership style?

4. How can a leader's personal history influence and impact their approach and attitude about leadership?

5. What benefits can leaders draw from their effective use of technology, presentation, and style?

6. FDR enjoyed unusually positive relations with the press during his long tenure. How did this relationship benefit his presidency? How can leaders establish positive working relationships with local media outlets in order to benefit their organizations?

✳ ✳ ✳

CASE 4: POWER STRUGGLE

John Tyler (1841-45)

It was a cold, rainy, and windy day as William Henry Harrison began what would become the longest Inaugural speech in U.S. history at one hour and forty minutes. At the age of 68, Harrison was the oldest president to take office at that point, and he wished to show his vitality by refusing to wear an overcoat or hat during the long speech. He caught a cold that day that grew into pneumonia when he went walking in wintry slush three weeks later. Within a week he was dead, the first president to die in office in the fifty-year history of the nation. He had served exactly one month.

Because the country had never faced an unscheduled presidential vacancy, no one was clear on the proper course of action. Article II of the Constitution merely stated that upon the death of a president, the office "will devolve on the vice president." Many of the leading officials in Congress interpreted this to mean that the vice president would serve as interim president until a new election could be held. As Congress debated this issue for the next several days, Vice President John Tyler boldly ignored the debate and had himself sworn in, delivered a brief Inaugural address, and moved into the executive mansion.

Senator Henry Clay and Secretary of State Daniel Webster attempted to dominate Tyler by asserting that the Cabinet would make all recommendations to Congress, which would then approve them. At the first meeting of the Cabinet since Harrison's death, Tyler rose and rebuked his secretary of state: "I am the president and I shall be held responsible for my administration. I can never consent to be dictated to. If you think otherwise, your resignation will be accepted." He went on to inform Congress that he was the legitimate and lawful president with all of the powers of the office as if he had been elected directly.

Congress, led by Senator Clay, was enraged. Calling Tyler "His Accidency," many members of Congress and the public began regularly protesting outside the White House, even burning the president in effigy. They refused to recognize the president's declaration of constitutional legitimacy and vowed to fight him for power. A crisis erupted when Sen. Clay and the Whig Party pushed for the re-chartering of the Bank of the United States. President Tyler vetoed the bill and when faced with a second similar measure, he once again applied a veto. As a result, Tyler's entire Cabinet resigned with the exception of Secretary of State Webster. The president immediately appointed new Cabinet officers through "recess appointments" made outside of Congress's scheduled session. The Cabinet crisis caused the Whig Party, to which the president was a member, to expel him from their ranks, rendering him without a political party.

Several months later, Congress sent President Tyler a series of protective tariff bills, all of which were vetoed as a matter of principle and a gesture of good will for ordinary citizens.

This latest display of power brought an angry mob one night to the executive mansion. Shouting insults at the president, the mob threw rocks at the mansion's windows, breaking several, and endangering Tyler's family. Fortunately, armed bodyguards thwarted the conflict. For the first time in history, though, an article of impeachment was introduced in Congress charging the president with misusing his veto authority. The Senate soundly dismissed the charges and Tyler remained in office until the end of his term. Upon visiting the beleaguered chief executive in 1842, Charles Dickens commented that "He looked worn and anxious. And well he might, being at war with everyone." Yet he managed to survive four difficult years in office, thereby setting an important precedent that future vice presidents have followed on the occasion of presidential death.

* * *

Library of Congress

Former President John Tyler as he prepared to take his seat
in the newly formed Confederate Congress, 1861

Case 4 Reflection

1. John Tyler did not wait for Congress to debate his legitimacy as president, despite the constitutional questions surrounding the nature of presidential succession. Why were these initial actions an important step in solidifying his authority?

2. Why is it important for leaders to "front load" their expectations and boundaries as leaders?

3. What can occur when leaders do not clearly solidify their authority early on?

4. President Tyler was expected to build consensus with his Cabinet, according to the expectations of Sen. Clay and Secretary of State Webster. Why did he refuse to submit to this form of leadership despite his limited political support?

5. When should leaders employ consensus building and when should they not? What are some examples of each?

6. President Tyler brought grace and dignity to the office while also standing firm in the wake of sometimes dangerous political events. How can these qualities be transferred to any organizational leadership role?

7. Why is it critical for leaders to remain steadfast, at least publicly, during explosive situations?

✳ ✳ ✳

CASE 5: GOING DOWN FIGHTING

Woodrow Wilson (1913-21)

The year was 1919 and the world had just witnessed the most widespread and deadly war in history up until that time. Drawn into the Great War in 1917 after campaigning on a platform of isolationism and peace, President Woodrow Wilson reluctantly, yet successfully, steered the nation and the Allied Powers towards victory. Arriving in Paris for the peace conference, Wilson was greeted by the largest crowds in human history, hailed as the "Savior of Humanity." Despite this greeting, he battled for three months with French Premier Georges Clemenceau and British Prime Minister David Lloyd George on the terms of peace, favoring a conciliatory settlement that included a mechanism for preventing future conflict. The cornerstone of the president's proposal was a "League of Nations" to serve as a "single overwhelming powerful group of nations who shall be the trustee of the peace of the world."

Eventually, Wilson convinced his European counterparts to stand behind the League. He returned to the United States in the spring of 1919 determined to secure his nation's ratification of the peace treaty in order to ensure that the Great War had truly been "the war to end all wars." The President personally delivered the treaty to the Senate, but was met at the door by his rival Henry Cabot Lodge, the majority leader. Sen. Lodge asked, "Mr. President, may I carry the treaty for you?" "Not on your life," replied Wilson. Sen. Lodge stalled a vote on the treaty for several months, and by summer it was apparent that the Senate would not vote for the treaty (or the League of Nations) as it was proposed.

The president decided to take his case directly to the American people in hopes of rallying popular support for the League that would, in turn, pressure senators to vote favorably. He embarked on an extensive cross-country train tour in which he gave 40 speeches in just 21 days, most of them in the hot late summer heat. In Oakland, Wilson sounded almost prophetic: "Little children are my real clients; there will be another and final war just about the time these children come to maturity." Addressing a crowd of 30,000 in San Diego, the president gave what one contemporary thought was among the most eloquent speeches in history. Wilson chastised the Senate for betraying "the sacrifices of mothers of sons who laid down their lives for an idea, for an ideal, for the only thing that is worth living for-the spiritual redemption that rests in the hearts of humanity."

By the time he arrived in Pueblo, Colorado, the president was exhausted. Complaining of headaches, he suffered a thrombosis, or blood clot to the brain. The train sped back to Washington so he could rest, but two days later the President collapsed in the White House of a massive stroke which caused his left side to become paralyzed. For the next week, the president lay close to death in the Lincoln Bedroom. For two months, he could not fulfill the minimum duties of his office. He did not meet with his Cabinet for the next seven months nor appeared in public for the next year. Wilson's wife, Edith, refused all visitors for several weeks, allowing only his doctor and a couple of close advisors access to her husband. What would occur over the next several months would result in the most severe crisis of presidential disability in American history.

Once an active and visible leader, rumors began to surface as to the president's true condition. Some believed Wilson was a prisoner in the White House; others thought he had gone insane; still others claimed the president was dead. Senate Majority Leader Lodge and Sen. Albert Fall wished to discredit their rival and asked for a meeting with President Wilson in order to convince the Senate that he was unfit for office. In response, Mrs. Wilson and the president's doctor devised an elaborate scheme to trick the senators when they visited the White House. Sen. Fall remarked as he was leaving, "Mr. President, I am praying for you," to which the president responded, "Which way, Senator?" The scheme worked, and no serious effort to remove Wilson from office was entertained in Congress.

As the months wore on, Secretary of State Lansing called a Cabinet meeting without Wilson's approval to discuss urgent matters. The president promptly fired him and the government continued to falter for the next 18 months without its leader. Many began to believe that Mrs. Wilson had become the de facto president as she controlled all correspondence and matters of state that were presented to her husband. There was speculation that she herself, and not the president, signed bills into law without her husband's knowledge. One senator remarked that Mrs. Wilson's power had created a "petticoat government" as a woman now sat at the head of the government. But the most tragic aspect of President Wilson's illness was his inability to exercise leadership with regards to the League of Nations and the peace treaty's ratification. Many senators expressed an interest in voting for the treaty and League if the president would make concessions. Instead, probably due to his stroke's effect, the president refused to compromise and the treaty was ultimately rejected by the Senate. Without the United States in the League, it was doomed from the start and President Wilson's prophetic warning of a second world war would in deed come true just twenty years later.

The president slowly improved over the year and a half until his term ended in 1921. But he never fully regained the energy or capacity to effectively serve as the Chief Executive. In time, he would go for short car rides with his wife that would end in embarrassment, such as tipping his hat to an empty sidewalk or insisting that his driver arrest a speeder. Visiting the White House in 1920, presidential candidate James Cox sobbed when he saw how the stroke had robbed the once vital president of the leadership the nation so desperately needed. As a result, Wilson's party was defeated in a landslide victory that year and the president interpreted this as a rejection of his ideas and principles. He was so sick on Inauguration Day in 1921 that he was unable to attend his successor's ceremony. He left the presidency a broken man whose idealistic pleas for an insurance policy that would prevent future wars went unheard. Had he been well, he may have convinced the United States to take an active role in peace and thus reduce the likelihood of World War II.

Case 5 Reflection

1. President Wilson sought to gain support for a League of Nations by appealing directly to the American people through a stringent train tour of the country. At what point must a leader bypass the normal channels of leadership and seek wider support for initiatives?

2. Woodrow Wilson has been described as one of the most skillful orators in U.S. history. Why must a leader have exemplary speaking skills?

3. The president's incapacitating disability was guarded carefully from the public. In the arena of leadership, at what point does it become necessary to remove a leader who may not be able to fulfill the duties of their position?

4. President Wilson's wife has often been referred to as the first female president in U.S. history due to her role in running the government after her husband became ill. In the absence of leadership, what often occurs and why?

5. Wilson paid a high price for his idealistic beliefs in the end, mostly because he was unable to compromise on the League of Nations. Why is the art of compromising so critical to leadership success?

6. How can leaders test the political waters to ensure that their initiatives are not outside the realm of reality with key stakeholders?

Library of Congress

President Woodrow Wilson with wife, Edith Wilson, 1920

* * *

CASE 6: UPHOLDING THE RULE OF LAW

Dwight D. Eisenhower (1953-61)

By the 1950s, civil rights for African-Americans was taking center stage as a major national issue. In 1954, Chief Justice Earl Warren and a majority of the U.S. Supreme Court handed down a watershed decision in Brown v. Board of Education, declaring that "separate but equal" facilities in education were unconstitutional. Effectively, the court's action forced the integration of all public schools in the nation with "all deliberate speed."

In response to the court's decision, the Little Rock, Arkansas, school board unanimously adopted a gradual integration plan for its city's schools. The plan was put into effect beginning in September 1957, starting with Central High School, an all-white school at that time. The NAACP sought to enroll nine African-American students at the high school on September 4, the first day of classes. An angry mob of white people met the students, taunting them and threatening violence. Gov. Orval Faubus responded by sending out the Arkansas National Guard to prevent the students from entering the high school and personally stood in the school's entrance to symbolically resist their efforts. Two weeks later, Gov. Faubus yielded to a court order to dismantle the National Guard's presence at Central High, but he did nothing to disperse the growing and increasingly hostile mob stationed at the school. As a result, the nine black students continued to be denied access to the school.

Pressure began mounting on President Dwight D. Eisenhower to respond to the crisis. Dr. Martin Luther King Jr., the civil rights leader, wrote the president that without federal action it would "set the process of integration back fifty years." Gov. Faubus's lack of support in restoring law and order in Little Rock caused the city's mayor to appeal directly to the president for help, declaring that the "situation is out of control." Furthermore, international pressure and attention was adding to the tensions, as many nations sympathized with the plight of African-Americans and were disgusted by the lack of federal action. Secretary of State John Foster Dulles warned the president that "this situation is ruining our foreign policy."

President Eisenhower privately did not agree with the Supreme Court's decision in *Brown v. Board of Education*, feeling that "the fellow who tries to tell me that you can do these things by force is just plain nuts." The president subscribed to the balance of federal and states' rights, and felt that integration of public facilities should be handled solely by states themselves. Furthermore, when pressure began building for his intervention in the crisis, Eisenhower cautiously answered, "I cannot imagine any set of circumstances that would ever induce me to send federal troops" to the South. In the meantime, he and Gov. Faubus met privately in

Rhode Island September 14 to attempt a resolution to the crisis. Eisenhower tried to persuade the governor to change the orders of the National Guard to preserving order and allowing for the safe passage of the students into Central High.

Though compliant in their private meeting, Gov. Faubus chose in the end to ignore the president. On September 23, President Eisenhower appealed directly to the mob in front of Central High, issuing a proclamation for them to disperse by the next day. On September 24, the nine students once again attempted to approach the school only to be turned away by the unruly mob. Finally, President Eisenhower realized he had exhausted all peaceful means to end the crisis, and went on national television that night to address the country about the crisis in Little Rock. He asserted, "the foundation of our American way of life is our national respect for law. The interest of the nation in the proper fulfillment of the law's requirements cannot yield to opposition and demonstration by some few persons." The president then addressed his constitutional obligations, maintaining that "the very basis of our individual rights and freedom rests upon the certainty that the president and executive branch of government will support and insure the carrying out of decisions of the federal courts, even, when necessary with all the means at the president's command."

He then immediately federalized the Arkansas National Guard and sent one thousand soldiers from the 101st Airborne Division to Little Rock. The next day, the soldiers surrounded Central High School and peacefully escorted the nine African-American students to classes after permanently dispersing the mob which had been at the school for three weeks. President Eisenhower kept a contingency of soldiers at the high school for the rest of the school year to protect the nine students. Upon being assisted by the long arm of the armed forces at the direction of its Commander-in-Chief, the President of the United States, one of the nine students remarked, "For the first time in my life, I feel like an American citizen." The crisis was over; the federal government had intervened to uphold the supremacy of the rule of law. Like some of his predecessors before him, Dwight Eisenhower was cautious about using power for its own sake. But he recognized its inherent value, and perhaps its obligatory necessity, when protecting the Constitution's cornerstone of rule by law.

❋ ❋ ❋

Case 6 Reflection

1. President Eisenhower wrestled with his response to the Little Rock crisis in 1957, partly due to his strong beliefs about limited federal government and the ability of states to act within their police powers without interference. What changed his mind?

2. President Eisenhower was known to be a cautious leader who resisted sweeping acts and responses. How did this approach hinder or help in the Little Rock case?

3. Historians believe that the president finally acted out of disgust for the defiant and insubordinate actions of Gov. Faubus and the angry mob that camped out at Central High School. How did Eisenhower's response to this flagrant defiance mirror the actions leaders must take when dealing with similar incidents?

4. When is it time for a leader to use the power of their position to right a wrong?

5. Leaders are routinely faced with crisis situations that can spin out of control in a short period of time. How did President Eisenhower's handling of the Little Rock crisis escalate or diffuse the situation? Would you have done the same or differently?

※ ※ ※

CASE 7: STRATEGIC GOVERNANCE

James K. Polk (1845-49)

James K. Polk was the nation's first "dark horse" candidate, elected in 1844 on a platform to expand the country's borders beyond the Mississippi River. Defeating better-known candidate Sen. Henry Clay, Polk vowed early on to serve a single term in office and he kept that promise. Knowing he had marked his own tenure, the new president confided in historian George Bancroft that he had four overarching goals that he intended to fulfill. His goals included reducing the tariff, creating an independent treasury, settling the long-disputed Oregon boundary, and acquiring California. His last goal inspired the journalist John O'Sullivan to declare that "nothing must interfere with the fulfillment of our manifest destiny to overspread the continent allotted by Providence." Polk would become the instrument of this surging nationalism.

President Polk used his influence and the large majorities of Democrats in Congress to push through his first two goals in the form of the Walker Tariff Act and the Independent Treasury Act in 1846. The third goal required more focused attention, as Oregon's boundary was a matter of dispute between the U.S. and Great Britain. Thousands of Americans had migrated to Oregon and Polk decided to try negotiating with Britain for the contested property. When Britain refused his offer, Polk broke off talks and played hard ball, asserting that "the only way to treat John Bull is to look him straight in the eye." The president threatened to take all of Oregon territory by force, whereby England then agreed to settle on the issue rather than fight another war with the U.S. Polk acquired large amounts of new land through a treaty signed in 1846, pushing the northern boundary to the 49th parallel.

Having met three of his strategic goals in less than two years, the president turned his attention to his most ambitious venture, the acquisition of California from Mexico. Mexico, though, had no interest in negotiating with the United States over this issue, rejecting Polk's envoy and offer of $20 million for the sought land. Annoyed by Mexico's lack of response to his proposal, President Polk sent troops to the contentious border between the two countries, thought to be the Rio Grande River by the United States government. Mexico considered troops deployed in the disputed area to be a violation of their sovereignty and retaliated against American forces led by Gen. Zachary Taylor. Though having provoked Mexico, President Polk told Congress that "war exists" and that "Mexico has passed the boundary of the United States, has invaded our country, and shed American blood on American soil." Congress promptly funded a war effort.

To realize his fourth strategic goal, the president developed three cornerstone war strategies: remove all Mexicans from Texas and occupy the northern provinces of Mexico; take possession of not only California, but also New Mexico; and seize control of Mexico City, the capital, to force surrender. The United

States army easily defeated Mexico and began the deliberations of peace. President Polk sent his envoy, Nicholas Trist, to protect the government's interests. Trist ended up ignoring his boss when in Mexico City, successfully negotiating a $15 million settlement that included Mexico ceding all land in present-day California and New Mexico. Though Polk angrily fired Trist for insubordination, he accepted the peace treaty as it had accomplished his fourth strategic goal.

James K. Polk had once called himself the "hardest working man in the country." During his four-year tenure, he was away from his desk less than any other American president, scarcely six weeks total, including vacations. President Polk even questioned the need for a Cabinet, asserting once that "I have become so familiar with the duties and workings of the government in both general principles and minute details that I find little difficulty in doing this." This detail-oriented management style kept Polk up until the early hours of the night as he worked on the affairs of state, earning him the distinction of being "an obsessive workaholic, a perfectionist, a micromanager." Polk's own secretary of state, James Buchanan, observed that his boss "was the most laborious man I have ever known; and in a brief period of four years had assumed the appearance of an old man." In fact, he worked so hard while in office that Polk died merely three months after the conclusion of his term at the age of fifty-three.

❊ ❊ ❊

Case 7 Reflection

1. Historian George Bancroft eulogized President Polk by describing him as "one of the very best and most honest and most successful presidents the country ever had." What accounted for his success?

2. President Polk utilized the processes of strategic planning upon entering office. How does this leadership and management style produce results? How can organizational leaders use this tool to further their goals?

3. President Harry Truman observed that James K. Polk "said exactly what he was going to do and he did it." How important is this skill when relating to organizational leadership?

4. How does a leader develop credibility with various constituents?

5. President Polk utilized micro management techniques as a management tactic. Debate the merits and drawbacks of using this approach to leadership.

6. In tackling organizational goals, is it more prudent to start with the toughest goals or the easiest ones? Why or why not? How did Polk approach his goals for the nation?

CASE 8: SEEKING COMMON GROUND

Richard M. Nixon (1969-74)

The Vietnam War had taken its toll on the nation by May of 1970. It had claimed the lives of tens of thousands of soldiers and destroyed as many families. The war had forced one president, Lyndon B. Johnson, from office and was beginning to destroy the presidency of his successor, Richard Nixon. At Kent State University, four students were killed when National Guardsmen opened fire on Vietnam War protesters, causing shockwaves across colleges and universities. By May 9, five days after Kent State, thousands of student protesters had descended on Washington, D.C., many camping out in the national monuments. Buses lined the streets around the White House with protesters, picketing for peace every hour of the day and night. The 82nd Airborne division of the Air Force was stationed across from the White House in order to protect the president and his family.

Times were tough, and the war had broken many people. Unable to sleep in the early morning hours of May 9, President Nixon chose to make fifty phone calls to various officials regarding the war, including eight calls to his secretary of state, Henry Kissinger. Gazing out a White House window around 4:00 a.m., the president could see protesters gathering at the Washington Monument, preparing for a new day full of demonstrations against him and his administration's handling and initial escalation of the war. After Kent State, some of these protesters had even called for the president's impeachment.

President Nixon asked his valet to accompany him for a visit to the Lincoln Memorial, with only a small number of Secret Service officers aware that he was leaving the White House. He made it clear that no administration official, nor the press, was to be alerted to his nighttime excursion, and from there his valet drove him to the Lincoln Memorial. Arriving at 4:40 am, at first the president merely showed his valet around the monument. After a couple of minutes, eight protesters who were asleep on the floor awoke and recognized the president, who began to engage them in conversation. President Nixon sought to connect with them about the war after some small talk, first explaining to the students that he was a Quaker by religion and was raised a pacifist. The president repeatedly explained that he wished the war was over as much as the students, and that he wished to "stop the killing, end the war, to bring peace."

By this point, the crowd around the president had grown and become more vocal. One protester angrily reported, "I hope you realize that we're willing to die for what we believe in." President Nixon responded, "I know that probably most of you think I'm an SOB. But I want you to know that I understand just how you feel." Though he attempted further discourse around the war and the meaning of the sacrifice the nation was making, most of his audience had become silent. The president then attempted to promote mutual understanding, talking about college, football, surfing, and foreign travel. Later, the press would interview the protesters about this strange meeting and find that they viewed the president's exchanges as "irrelevant" and "flippant."

As the crowd around him grew in size, the president's staff began to fear for his safety. His limited Secret Service detail was visibly agitated, and President Nixon would later recount that "I have never seen the Secret Service quite so petrified with apprehension." After all, it had been less than seven years since the assassination of President Kennedy, so any potential threat to a president was cause for alarm. Having been with the protesters for 45 minutes, the world's most powerful man noticed the sun rising on the monument and knew that his presence would attract hordes of additional protesters.

Shaking hands with several students nearby him, he turned and walked to his limousine and promptly left the grounds. Instead of returning to the White House, the president took his valet to the Capitol where they found an empty building, save for custodial staff. Nixon sat at his old seat in the House of Representatives and instructed his valet to approach the rostrum and deliver a short speech to the empty room. They went to a local restaurant for breakfast before heading back to the White House. Thus ended one of the strangest episodes in American presidential history.

* * *

Case 8 Reflection

1. President Nixon ignored standard security protocols in order to seek common ground with those hostile to his policies. What were his motives for doing so?

2. The presidency can isolate leaders from the real issues facing the public. Many presidents have sought to circumvent this isolation. Can you think of parallels that trap organizational leaders?

3. Though a largely effective speaker in front of crowds, President Nixon was known to be awkward in more informal settings. How can this be detrimental to a leader's effectiveness?

4. Consider an occasion where a leader was faced with a serious issue that was all-consuming. How was it resolved both formally and informally?

5. How can unorthodox problem-solving strategies be beneficial?

6. Put yourself in President Nixon's shoes. Would you have met directly with the protesters?

7. Weigh the pros and cons of passive vs. aggressive response patterns when confronted by conflict. Which one is more effective, and dominant, in your estimation?

IT'S 2AM AT 1600 PENNSYLVANIA AVENUE

Bettmann-Getty Images

President Richard Nixon with Vietnam War protesters
at the Lincoln Memorial, May 1970

✻ ✻ ✻

CASE 9: ACT OF JUSTICE, PART A

Abraham Lincoln (1861-65)

Much has been written about Abraham Lincoln and his extraordinary grip on history. Rising from poverty to the highest office in the land and governing during the most divisive events ever to plague the United States, Lincoln has been scrutinized for every act he made as president. Many have criticized the seemingly hesitant manner in which he finally came to free the nation's slaves, the one act for which his name will never be forgotten.

By the time Abraham Lincoln took the oath of office in March 1861, most of the southern states had already seceded from the Union and thus did not recognize his authority as the national leader. Extending an olive branch, the new president invited the southern leaders to return to the Union without retribution, asserting that he had no intention of abolishing slavery nor did he feel he had the legal ability to do so. "In your hands, my fellow countrymen, is the momentous issue of civil war," a statement that was answered a month later when Fort Sumter was seized by the Confederacy.

Despite the next two years of bloody battles and thousands of lives lost, President Lincoln refused to consider emancipation of the slaves and thus kept his focus on keeping the nation together. He was resolved to use "all indispensable means" to preserve the Union, resisting "radical" measures for fear of offending the loyal Border States, which could tip the war in the South's direction. The president went so far as to forbid his military officers to free slaves when capturing southern territory during battle. He further upheld the controversial Fugitive Slave Act that required northern states to return runaway slaves to their southern masters. Lincoln tried in earnest to compromise with Congress by presenting two ill-fated plans for consideration during the long years of 1861-62. One plan involved rounding up millions of African-Americans and colonizing them in Central America or the Caribbean under the protection of the U.S. government. Still another bill was introduced to gradually emancipate slaves over a decade through monetary compensation to slaveholding states. Neither plan won enough support from Congress or the Border States and were quickly set aside.

For these desperate acts, Frederick Douglass reflected that "Mr. Lincoln seemed tardy, cold, dull, and indifferent" to the slavery issue. Abolitionists across the North attacked the president in newspapers for his failure to act, some questioning if the president was a racist and Confederate sympathizer. Prominent Massachusetts Republican Francis Bird went so far as to lament that "the key to the slaves' chain is now kept in the White House." One hundred years later in 1968, civil rights advocate Julius Lester observed from afar that President Lincoln's "pen was sitting on his desk the whole time" and that he had no excuse but to have destroyed slavery once war broke out in 1861.

By the fall of 1862, though, President Lincoln returned to his deeply ingrained hatred of slavery and began to create a dual purpose for the horrific Civil War to which the nation was then engaged. Despite his reluctance to alienate the Border States and many northern politicians who wanted nothing to do with emancipation, Lincoln quietly consulted his closest advisors about the possibility of a presidential decree of emancipation. But again he faltered when a series of battles in the fall of 1862 further eroded the North's military capacity to fight and win the war. He viewed a declaration of emancipation amongst the military failures as a desperate attempt to win the war through propaganda. A draft of the Emancipation Proclamation would go into a desk drawer to be ignored for several more weeks.

※ ※ ※

IT'S 2AM AT 1600 PENNSYLVANIA AVENUE

Alexander Gardner

President Abraham Lincoln aged rapidly in office

Case 9 Reflection

1. The first two years of Abraham Lincoln's administration were spent focused on keeping the fractured nation together. Lincoln gave very little attention to the issue of slavery, to which he is best known today. What consequences resulted from following this course?

2. President Lincoln had explored several possibilities for solving the slavery question in his early years in office before his Emancipation Proclamation. Given the times to which he governed, were his strategies defensible?

3. Organizational leaders are faced with paradoxical scenarios regularly and must act in the best interests of the greater good. What example can you consider that would fit this leadership test?

4. President Lincoln was a cautious and thoughtful leader who considered many options available before taking action. How is this both an asset and a liability?

5. Most historians agree that Abraham Lincoln, while alive, was the most vilified president in history. How can leaders weather strife in order to achieve resiliency?

6. Lincoln was criticized heavily by abolitionists, even labeled a racist, for his slow response to slavery. How can leaders respond when they are unfairly accused?

※ ※ ※

CASE 10: ACT OF JUSTICE, PART B

Abraham Lincoln (1861-65)

At the beginning of the Civil War, President Abraham Lincoln viewed the conflict as a struggle to keep the nation together. Though he personally was repulsed by slavery, the president did not consider this a motive for the war. In fact, he did everything he could to appease the South before Fort Sumter, including promises to maintain the "peculiar institution" of slavery. He held that "all indispensable means" must be afforded to hold the states together, thereby resisting any "radical" and sweeping measures that would alter the status quo. After Fort Sumter, he remained largely silent on the issue for almost two years so as to not alienate the Border States and cause them to leave the Union. He believed that his oath to uphold the Constitution only commanded him to preserve the nation, not destroy the legally sanctioned institution that was the basis of decades of strife between North and South.

But by the fall of 1862, President Lincoln realized that the bloody war that would eventually claim over 600,000 lives must have a moral purpose beyond the Union's existence. To this end,

Lincoln began turning to God for guidance, "deeply sensible of his need of Divine assistance to handle the slavery issue." He became convinced that he was called to do His work, to right the wrongs that had shamefully shackled millions of human beings. He waited for a moment of military strength after the North had won a decisive battle and then made his announcement to free slaves in those states still in rebellion on January 1, 1863. In essence, this Emancipation Proclamation freed not one slave because its application pertained to states that did not recognize Lincoln's authority. Because it was a unilateral presidential decree without Congressional backing, Lincoln derived its lawfulness in his powers as Commander-in-Chief, finding it "a military necessity, absolutely necessary to the preservation of the Union."

New Year's Day came and with it 500 guests at the White House. The exhausted president shook hands for hours before retiring to his study with Cabinet officers for the signing of the document. His hand was numb from all of the hand shaking and he trembled as he lifted the pen for his signature. Suddenly, a sense of calm came over him and he steadily signed his full name, one of the few occasions he did not use shorthand, declaring "if my name ever goes into history, it will be for this act." Later, he would recount privately that he felt the hand of God Himself hold his own hand as he signed the Emancipation Proclamation. "I never, in my life, felt more certain that I was doing right, than I do signing this paper." He considered this document, though of no actual consequence at that moment, to be the inevitable act of justice by which a new chapter in American history would be written. His assertion that the United States could no longer endure "half slave and half free" finally met action on that cold January day.

The border states remained silent on the proclamation as it

did not free any slaves within their borders. Reaction in the North was mixed, but at first many despised the president's act as illegal. In New York City, draft riots broke out to protest this new war purpose. Angry residents burned down the draft office, attacked the mayor's house, beat blacks to death, and killed police officers. After five hundred residents died from the rioting, the governor of New York demanded that Lincoln repeal the proclamation and suspend the draft. He was attacked in the press as a tyrant and many believed he would never be reelected in 1864 because of this act. But the president had toughened over the years, and he met the criticism with his defense that "those who deny freedom to others deserve it not for themselves, and under a just God cannot long retain it." He refused to repeal the Emancipation Proclamation or suspend the draft, observing that "I may be a slow walker, but I never walk backward."

Lincoln knew that the Emancipation Proclamation was merely a temporary order that could be overturned by a future president or act of Congress. After he was reelected in 1864, President Lincoln moved swiftly to ensure that the 13th Amendment to the Constitution be enacted to outlaw slavery for all time. Upon its passage on January 31, 1865, long-time critic and abolitionist William Lloyd Garrison declared joyfully that Lincoln was the "presidential chain-breaker for millions of the oppressed." In his second Inaugural Address a month later, the Great Emancipator attacked slavery as "a sin in the sight of God" and vowed to fight for voting rights for blacks as the nation began the long road to healing and "binding up the nation's wounds." Shortly after he was sworn in for a second term, the Confederacy fell and Lincoln travelled to Richmond, the rebel capital. Thousands of freed blacks surrounded the president as he walked unguarded through the streets of Richmond. One slave sobbed, "I know I am free, for I have seen Father Abraham." The president redirected this praise, pointing to Heaven as he said, "Do not kneel to me. You must kneel to God only and thank Him for your liberty."

More than anything else, though, it was President Lincoln's stance against slavery that resulted in national tragedy just six days after the surrender of southern troops to General Ulysses Grant. On April 14, 1865, white supremacist and noted actor John Wilkes Booth slipped into the presidential box at Ford's Theater and shot Lincoln to death as revenge for abolishing slavery. Walt Whitman, a contemporary poet, summed up the grief that overcame even those who had deplored the president and everything he stood for while he was alive: "O Captain, my Captain! Our fearful trip is done; the ship has weathered every rock, the prize we sought is won. But O heart! Heart! Heart! O the bleeding drops of red, where on the deck my Captain lies, fallen, cold, and dead." Despised, hated, and vilified in life, President Abraham Lincoln followed his heart and led the nation through its most destructive crisis. In death, his righteousness and force of conviction became apparent and remain a source of example and strength for all Americans.

❉ ❉ ❉

Case 10 Reflection

1. At first, the Emancipation Proclamation was merely a symbolic gesture that did not accomplish its objective. When and why should leaders take action when they know the action may be of no substantive value?

2. How did Lincoln's faith play a role in his eventual decision to issue the Emancipation Proclamation? Does faith play a role in leadership?

3. Explain the essence of Lincoln's statement, "I may be a slow walker, but I never walk backward."

4. President Lincoln was steadfast in his resolution to defend the Emancipation, refusing to rescind it despite serious opposition and violent backlash. How is this a vital component of leadership effectiveness?

5. How can changes in leadership amidst a crisis be traumatic for an organization?

6. Can you think of a leader whose tenure was rocky while in office, but whose legacy has improved the memory of this individual?

* * *

CASE 11: CAMELOT

John F. Kennedy (1961-63)

In his hit 1976 song, "She is Always Seventeen," Harry Chapin memorialized President John F. Kennedy through these words: "It was 1961 when we went to Washington...we listened to his visions of how our land should be...we gave him our hearts and minds...then we heard what happened in that brutal Dallas light." The first president to use television as a tool to win election to the White House, Kennedy understood its potential and used it to build and solidify his long-lasting grip on the American public. Elected by the smallest margin in American history, what is even more profound is that he beat a better-known incumbent vice president. He took the oath of office at the age of 43, declaring in his Inaugural Address on January 20, 1961, that "the torch has been passed to a new generation of Americans."

Almost immediately, he became the idol of young people in both the nation and the world. His relative youth and idealism, coupled with his young family, brought a new sense of energy and inspiration to public service and government. Prior to Kennedy's election, college-aged students had been labeled the "silent generation." Within two years of his taking office, JFK's introduction of a Peace Corps program changed this apathy and caused 5,000 young Americans to enlist in the Peace Corps. Interest in civil service positions skyrocketed during Kennedy's presidency. The young president capitalized on his magnetic pull with the people by holding 64 news briefings in just three years in office. His wit and charm contributed to the large audiences that would tune into these briefings, sometimes as high as 60 million viewers.

When the Soviet Union launched the first man in space in 1961, JFK cleverly ignored this feat and instead focused on the future. Within a year, the United States had replicated this event when John Glenn was launched into space. He declared in a major policy speech that "I believe that this nation should commit itself to achieving the goal, before this decade is out, of landing a man on the moon and returning him safely to the earth." This dream was realized in 1969 when Neil Armstrong walked on the moon. The president's commitment and inspirational words took a dream and made it a reality. JFK reminded the nation that exploratory adventures should not be done because "they are easy, but because they are hard."

Though reluctant early in his administration to take on the momentous issue of civil rights for African-Americans, Kennedy became more convinced throughout his term that civil rights needed to be dealt with head on. On June 11, 1963, when two students attempted to enroll at the University of Alabama, Gov. George Wallace physically stood in the doorway to bar them from entering the school. President Kennedy sent federal marshals along with the National Guard to force Wallace from the doorway and allow the students to be enrolled. That same night, JFK went on live national television to promote a strong bill sent to Congress that would equalize the rights of all Americans. In this speech, the president observed that "One hundred years of delay have passed since President Lincoln freed the slaves, yet their heirs... are not yet freed from the bonds of injustice." The bill stalled in Congress for several months and was finally passed at the urging of President Johnson in 1964 as a memorial to the slain president.

President Kennedy had long been a cold warrior who held much skepticism of the Soviet Union and its intentions. In order to affirm the freedom of all people and express his displeasure of the Berlin Wall, he traveled to West Berlin in June 1963. Riding in a motorcade through the divided city, JFK was cheered by two million residents, later appearing before a crowd of 100,000 people in which he delivered one of his most memorable speeches: "There are some who say that communism is the wave of the future. Let them come to Berlin. As a free man, I take pride in the words, 'Ich bin ein Berliner' (I am a Berliner)." Kennedy's defiance of the Soviet Union in the shadow of the Berlin Wall would inspire other American presidents to stand their ground in defense of freedom, including President Reagan who challenged Soviet leader Mikhail Gorbachev to "tear down this wall" twenty-five years later.

After President Kennedy's assassination in November 1963, his widow was interviewed regarding her husband's legacy. Jackie Kennedy revealed that JFK would often fall asleep to a song with the words, "Let it never be forgot that once there was a time called Camelot." Shortly after, the term Camelot began to be used to define the Kennedy presidency and its magical connection to the American people. President Kennedy brought a sense of style, grace, and youth to the most powerful office on Earth and used the mileage gained from this image to transform the political landscape for decades to come.

IT'S 2AM AT 1600 PENNSYLVANIA AVENUE

�֍ ✶ ✶

National Archives
JFK with his children Caroline and John Jr.

Case 11 Reflection

1. President Kennedy had a charismatic personality that captivated the American public. How can charisma be an essential ingredient in successful leadership?

2. JFK was a powerful public speaker who could rally millions by his oratory. How can leaders improve their public speaking abilities in order to advocate for reform?

3. Though slow to embrace civil rights, President Kennedy nonetheless came to regard it as a necessary area of his attention prior to his death. How can incidents or movements influence and shape the priorities of leaders?

4. How can regular communication mechanisms help connect leaders with those they lead? What examples are available to leaders to ensure this communication?

5. Many questioned the wisdom of JFK's goal to land a man on the moon within ten years. What examples can you think of where a leader articulated a goal that was outside the grasp of those being persuaded?

6. Consider the power of symbolism as a leadership tool. What are its useful qualities?

CASE 12: "FEAR NO EVIL"

George W. Bush (2001-09)

Few presidents have had to face a catastrophic series of events within a short period of time that threatened the imminent security of the United States. President George W. Bush was told by his chief of staff, Andrew Card, of the attacks on the World Trade Center on September 11, 2001, while he was reading to elementary school children in Sarasota, FL. Instead of abruptly leaving the classroom, the president finished reading to the children despite the knowledge that the nation had been brutally attacked by terrorists who used airplanes to destroy the WTC and parts of the Pentagon. Though his first instinct was to return to the White House, the Secret Service warned the president that Washington, D.C. also was being targeted, and possibly the White House itself. President Bush reluctantly flew to a secure bunker at Barksdale AFB in Louisiana, where he addressed the nation for the first time since the attacks. In this short speech, President Bush said "I want to reassure the American people that the full resources of the federal government are working...the resolve of our great nation is being tested. But make no mistake: We will show the world that we will pass this test. God Bless."

The president insisted on returning to the capital city later in the day so that he could address the nation from the Oval Office, as he knew this familiar symbol of power would be reassuring to Americans. "Terrorist attacks can shake the foundations of our biggest buildings, but they cannot touch the foundation of America. These acts shattered steel, but they cannot dent the steel of American resolve...We will make no distinction between the terrorists who committed these acts and those who harbor them... And I pray they will be comforted by a power greater than any of us, spoken through the ages in Psalm 23: Even though I walk through the valley of the shadow of death, I fear no evil, for You are with me...America has stood down enemies before, and we will do so this time."

The president wasted no time assembling his national security team for intense strategy sessions. He maintained constant communication with New York City Mayor Rudy Giuliani and New York Gov. George Pataki and enlisted the support of heads of state across the globe, most notably British Prime Minister Tony Blair. On September 13, President Bush was overwhelmed with emotion when addressing reporters in the Oval Office, declaring "I am also someone, however, who has a job to do, and I intend to do it. And this is a terrible moment." On September 14, he led the nation in a day of prayer along with four former presidents at the National Cathedral.

That same day, President Bush flew to New York City for the first time since the attacks. As he toured the destruction at Ground Zero, the nation's leader spontaneously climbed on top of a rubble pile that served as a makeshift stage. Using a megaphone to project his voice over the ruins, and draping his arm over a firefighter who was standing with him, the president was at first inaudible, prompting the crowd to shout, "We can't hear you!" The president responded, "I can hear you. The rest of the world hears you. And the people who knocked these buildings down will hear from all of us soon." He took time to comfort the grieving, including a mother whose son, a police officer, was killed in the destruction. The mother handed the president her son's police badge, and he proudly accepted it with a promise to keep it as a reminder of all those who perished in the terrorist attacks. President Bush would keep the officer's badge in his wallet as promised, and display it for the nation on numerous occasions.

The president monitored his national security team's intelligence gathering efforts and on September 17, just six days after 9/11, announced that terrorist leader Osama bin Laden was responsible for the attacks. At a press conference that day, the president resolved to bring bin Laden to justice "dead or alive." These remarks sealed his popular image as an American cowboy across the world, usually in less than flattering terms, but the president would make no apologies for his word choice. He began an exhaustive strategy to marginalize the terrorists, starting with an executive order freezing the assets of terrorist groups with accounts in the United States.

President Bush took immediate steps to federalize the nation's airport screening process, reopening airports after 9/11 with marshals trained and paid for by the government. He successfully advocated for the creation of a Department of Homeland Security, a Cabinet-level office, to coordinate all internal security within the nation's borders. The president proposed the Patriot Act, which Congress promptly passed, expanding police powers with increased surveillance of suspected terrorists. Later, the president would order retaliatory measures against Afghanistan and Iraq for their role in terrorist activity. Nine days after 9/11, President Bush appeared before a joint session of Congress in a defiant tone, with a stern warning: "Every nation now has a decision to make: Either you are with us, or you are with the terrorists." More importantly, the president prepared the nation for a new kind of war, one that would bring sacrifices. "Americans should not expect one battle, but a lengthy campaign, unlike any other we have ever seen. We'll meet violence with patient justice." Throughout his eight years in office, the president waged two wars and managed to thwart numerous attempts to attack the United States.

❊ ❊ ❊

Case 12 Reflection

1. President Bush was not known for being an eloquent speaker, but his responses in the aftermath of 9/11 are among the most heartfelt and genuine remarks ever uttered by an American president. How did his words comfort a nation?

2. President Bush was among the most religious leaders to ever serve the United States. How did his quote of Scripture on the evening of 9/11 strengthen his ability to reassure the nation after that day's horrific events?

3. How can the choice of words spoken in the wake of tragedy or urgent situations be of critical importance in the context of organizational leaders?

4. Consider the initial actions that leaders must take when responding to a crisis. Why are these actions of a critical nature?

5. Evaluate the differences between planned and impromptu leadership actions and speech.

6. President Bush did not waver on 9/11 or in the days following this tragedy. What characteristics define a steady leader?

JEFFREY J. PORTER

White House Photo Office

President George W. Bush at Ground Zero in New York City
after the terrorist attacks, September 2001

✸ ✸ ✸

CASE 13: ART OF DIPLOMACY

Ronald Reagan (1981-89)

In a 1983 speech, President Ronald Reagan warned, "Let us be aware that while the Soviet leaders preach the supremacy of the state, declare its omnipotence over individual man, and predict its eventual domination of all peoples on the earth, they are the focus of evil in the modern world." Reagan was a product of the Cold War and sharply reversed the 1970s diplomacy of detente, whereby conciliatory relations between the U.S. and Soviet Union were the norm. Now, President Reagan went on a campaign of harsh public words followed up by no private contact between the superpowers, markedly different from decades of uneasy relations. The president believed that any future negotiations with the Soviet Union must be conducted from a position of strength only, and felt that his immediate predecessors had allowed the U.S. to be weakened. To further his agenda, Reagan secretly deployed long-range intercontinental ballistic missiles in underground silos in direct violation of an earlier treaty.

During his first term, President Reagan was faced with regular leadership turnover at the Kremlin. When three Soviet leaders-

Brezhnev, Andropov, and Chernenko- died within a short period of time, the president expressed his frustration: "How am I supposed to get any place with the Russians if they keep dying on me?" Finally, Mikhail Gorbachev succeeded Chernenko as Soviet general secretary, and both leaders agreed to meet for a summit in Geneva, Switzerland, in November 1985. This first meeting went well and ended with the president and general secretary agreeing to two future summits. President Reagan began to have a change of heart towards the Soviet Union after the summit, confiding that he could work with Gorbachev due to his likable and practical nature.

A year later, the two leaders met for a second summit in Reykjavik, Iceland, in order to discuss possible reductions in nuclear arms. However, Gorbachev surprised Reagan with a series of bold proposals, including a 50% reduction in strategic missiles. Before the president had a chance to absorb Gorbachev's offer, the general secretary dropped a bombshell: eliminate all nuclear weapons within one decade on both sides and abandon the president's "Star Wars" program, his signature strategic defense initiative. Reagan knew that without nuclear weapons, the U.S. would be no match for the superiority of the Soviet Union's vast traditional armed forces. He also worried about a rogue nation gaining nuclear weapons technology and dominating the U.S. and Western Europe.

When Gorbachev insisted on his terms, President Reagan considered it a trick and stood up from the negotiating table in defiance of the Soviet leader. Angrily, he told Secretary of State George Shultz, "Let's go; we're leaving," and then abruptly left the summit. Neither leader communicated with each other for the next several months. The president would later reflect that the last day in Iceland was "one of the longest, most disappointing, and ultimately angriest days of my presidency." He reverted to his earlier policy of engaging the Soviet leaders in public only, icily provoking the general secretary at the Brandenburg Gate in West Berlin in June 1987, declaring "Mr. Gorbachev, tear down this wall!"

But President Reagan knew he must press for peace and considered Gorbachev to be the best chance he had to realize his goal of a nuclear-free world. Thus, Reagan invited the Soviet leader to the White House in December 1987 and both men agreed to sweeping changes in their own attitudes towards winning the Cold War. It was at this summit that they signed the INF Treaty, reducing 4% of all nuclear weapons on both sides. The president joked with his Soviet counterpart that the treaty would only work if both countries could "trust but verify" with independent on-site inspectors. Gorbachev agreed. The next summit occurred only five months later in Moscow this time. Instead of attacking Gorbachev as the leader of the "evil empire," Reagan referred to the Soviet chief as "my friend." Many have credited President Reagan's persistence and efforts in helping to accelerate the collapse of the Soviet Union within three years of him leaving office.

❋ ❋ ❋

Case 13 Reflection

1. President Reagan chose to ignore the Soviet leaders early in his presidency, instead turning to public rebukes against the Soviet Union without a plan to seek common ground. Why did he do this and was it effective?

2. Why did President Reagan change his approach to the Soviet Union? Why is it important for leaders to adjust their attitudes and stances towards those they must work with?

3. Relationships are at the heart of successful leadership. How can relationships improve the organizational environment?

4. Rhetoric is a leadership tool that can lead to successful change. What purpose did President Reagan hope to accomplish by challenging Premier Gorbachev at the Berlin Wall?

5. How, and when, should leaders use rhetoric to further their goals?

6. When is compromise the answer and when is it not?

7. President Reagan abruptly, and angrily, left the Iceland Summit after Mr. Gorbachev revealed conditions that were unacceptable to the president. At what times should leaders employ this strategy when a meeting is yielding poor results?

IT'S 2AM AT 1600 PENNSYLVANIA AVENUE

Wikimedia Commons

President Ronald Reagan and Soviet Premier Mikhail Gorbachev at the Oval Office, 1987

* * *

CASE 14: THE COMEBACK KID

Harry S Truman (1945-53)

President Harry S Truman had succeeded to the presidency upon the death of his predecessor, Franklin D. Roosevelt, and most of his contemporaries did not expect him to win the office in his own right. Truman's popularity dipped from 87% to 50% between 1945 and 1946, such that Republicans took control of both houses of Congress in the midterm elections in November 1946 with the slogan, "Had Enough?" A household saying during the president's first years in office was "To err is Truman" and this became the backdrop by which he began his bid for a term of his own in 1948. Thomas E. Dewey, the governor of New York, was again the Republican nominee that year as he had been in 1944, and most expected him to easily defeat Truman. In fact, Dewey himself came across as cool and calm throughout the campaign, taking care not to do anything to damage his enormous lead in the polls.

Described as a "gone goose," President Truman was repeatedly persuaded to drop out of the race during the primary season in order to allow a stronger candidate a chance to defeat Dewey in the general election. Truman refused, and the Democrats grudgingly re-nominated him after the party split off into three factions in order to accommodate pro-civil rights and anti-civil rights viewpoints. Presiding over a crumbling political party, the president tried to ignore the fact that "every seasoned Democratic leader is convinced that Harry Truman will suffer an historic defeat." A poll in September 1948 predicted a 44% to 31% lead for Dewey, concluding that any future polling was unnecessary due to the improbable belief that Truman could catch up with his challenger.

Fifty of the leading reporters of the day predicted defeat for the sitting president. Journalists in the fall of 1948 "spent most of their time speculating on the extent of Mr. Truman's defeat in November." *The New York Herald* printed: "Dewey...has the election in the bag." *The New York Star*: "It is three months to January 20, when Tom Dewey will, in all probability, move into the White House." *TIME Magazine*: "There is not much left to this presidential campaign except counting the votes." One leading newspaper's editorial page: "The election must be held for no other reason than to find out which national pollster comes the closest." President Truman would not accept the dire reports of his demise and set out during the fall months on a whistle-stop campaign tour by rail around the nation. Traveling 22,000 miles and giving an exhausting 270 speeches in just two months, historians estimate that he reached six million people on his tour. Pledging to "give 'em hell," the president ran against what he considered to be the "Do-Nothing Congress" that had refused to take action on any of his proposals.

On the day before the election, polls continued to show Dewey way ahead. The Gallup Poll gave Dewey a comfortable

50% to Truman's 45%. *The New York Times* predicted that Dewey would carry at least 26 states to Truman's 16 states, collecting 345 electoral votes to Truman's 105. The *Times* printed this the day before the election: "Thomas E. Dewey's election as president is a foregone conclusion." *LIFE Magazine* printed their cover with a photo of Dewey and labeled it with "The next President of the United States." Having already moved past the inevitable one day before the election, the *New York Herald Tribune* wrote: "Events will not wait patiently until Thomas E. Dewey officially replaces Harry S Truman."

On Election Day, the *Chicago Tribune* didn't wait for the results, instead printing its cover page with the headline "Dewey Defeats Truman," which was widely circulated and believed by voters. As the day dragged on, an amazing course of events began to unfold. President Truman took an early lead that he maintained throughout the night, finishing with 303 electoral votes to 189 for Dewey. Truman had won by more than two million votes, taking 28 states to Dewey's 16 states. On his coattails, both the House and Senate were returned to the Democrats in a year that was supposed to be exclusively Republican. It had become, without a doubt, the biggest political upset in U.S. history.

❋ ❋ ❋

IT'S 2AM AT 1600 PENNSYLVANIA AVENUE

Library of Congress

President Truman beat all Election Day forecasts in 1948

Case 14 Reflection

1. President Truman had every reason to give up early in 1948, rather than pursue a hopeless campaign. Why did he choose to forge ahead?

2. There are times when leaders must ignore the critics and do what they believe is right. What is at least one occasion that can illustrate this truth?

3. President Truman used a brilliant political tactic to produce traction during the election campaign by running against the "Do-Nothing" Congress. Why was this an important decision and how did it work in his favor?

4. Leaders can face resistance from all sectors of an organization when proposing reforms. In the face of the status quo, how can leaders build support that will ultimately prevail?

5. Leadership is a volatile and fast-changing roller coaster ride at times. How can resiliency be an important trait for leaders to adopt?

6. President Truman proved that the mainstream and popular attitudes towards issues and personalities can be misleading. How is this a valuable lesson for organizational leaders?

* * *

CASE 15: IN REVERENCE FOR THE OFFICE, PART A

James A. Garfield (1881)

James A. Garfield rose in protest at the 1880 Republican convention when his name was put forward as the compromise nominee for a party that was badly divided. The Stalwart faction of the party, which sought to continue patronage, and the Half-Breeds, who wished to reform government, were satisfied with Garfield's nomination because of the candidate's mixed record on reform amidst accusations of corruption in his earlier years. In order to carry the crucial state of New York, Garfield agreed to the demands of Sen. Roscoe Conkling, the corrupt "boss" of the political machinery of that state, that he appoint only those favorable to the senator. He won the election narrowly by meeting the demands of the Stalwart faction and Sen. Conkling.

Once in office, though, President Garfield immediately began to distance himself from the Stalwarts. He appointed James G. Blaine, leader of the Senate's Half-Breeds, as his secretary of state.

The new president backed his postmaster general's investigation of fraud, exposing powerful Republican politicians in his own party. When asked if he wanted to follow through on this investigation, the president remarked, "I have sworn to execute the laws. Go ahead, regardless of where or whom you hit." In 1881, the position of New York City customs collector was a highly prized partisan position and presidents had historically consulted Sen. Conkling before appointments were made for this position. Instead, Garfield ignored the senator and chose another candidate for the post, inciting the wrath of the Stalwart faction. Sen. Conkling fought back, but President Garfield was unyielding. "This will settle the question whether the president is the registering clerk of the Senate or the Executive of the United States." In the end, Garfield's choice was approved and Sen. Conkling abruptly resigned his Senate seat in disgrace.

Despite his early successes in fighting corruption, President Garfield was dogged by the endless procession of office-seekers, a common problem in the late 1800s. He complained about the long lines waiting outside his office: "I face disciplined office hunters, who draw papers on me as highwaymen draw pistols. These people would take my very brain, flesh, and blood, if they could." One office seeker was an unstable man named Charles Guiteau, who wished to be appointed consul in Paris, and Sec. of State Blaine had him banned from government offices, telling him "Never speak to me again on the Paris consulship as long as you live." He stalked the president regularly after this, even camping out across from the White House so that he could watch Garfield's movements. He wrote the president a letter that was dismissed as "insane," stating that "The president's tragic death was a sad necessity, but it will unite the Republican Party and save the Republic. His death was a political necessity."

On July 2, 1881, President Garfield arrived at Union Station in Washington with Secretary of State Blaine to board a train for a speaking engagement at Williams College. Guiteau came up behind the president and shot him twice at point blank range, striking him down as Garfield yelled, "My God, what is this?" Doctors rushed to the president's side as his would-be assassin was caught before he even left Union Station. President Garfield was taken back to the White House, where he was attended to by some of the finest doctors of that time, and their one objective was to remove the bullet lodged in his back. At first, the president's condition improved, with initial reports to the public promising. Three weeks later, in late July, he took a turn for the worse with fever, chills, and tremors, and doctors operated three times in order to fight infection. Crowds gathered outside the White House daily to pray for the president and seek information of his condition. Garfield's prognosis improved once again as the surgeries stabilized his fragile health.

But by early September, President Garfield insisted on leaving the intense heat of Washington, despite a crude air conditioning system that engineers had rigged to relieve his discomfort. He was moved by train to the seashore of New Jersey, where he found relief in the cool coastal air. Nine days after arriving at the shore, though, the president again succumbed to infection, and doctors this time were unable to help him. "My work is done," were his last words before he died on September 19, having served in office a mere four months. Yet President Garfield's brief battle against corruption and his subsequent assassination awakened the nation to the need for real reform in government.

Wikimedia Commons

Secretary of State James G. Blaine (left) reacts as President James A. Garfield is struck by an assassin's bullet July 2, 1881 at Union Station, Washington, D.C.

Case 15 Reflection

1. President Garfield gave assurances to Sen. Conkling and other Stalwarts during the campaign that he later retracted once he was elected. What is your observation of the frequency to which leaders will be deceptive in order to obtain positions of authority?

2. How would you evaluate President Garfield's showdown in the Senate with Sen. Conkling? Why was this an important event for the new president?

3. Once in office, James Garfield proved to be reform-minded. How can a leader's strong ethics contribute to the overall health of an organization?

4. What message does a leader send by the kinds of individuals he or she appoints to important and influential positions?

5. How does a leader balance the best interests of the organization with political realities and setbacks?

6. Reform can be rocky and controversial. How does a leader weather, and direct, the many challenges that accompany such unstable working conditions?

* * *

CASE 16: IN REVERENCE FOR THE OFFICE, PART B

Chester A. Arthur (1881-85)

Vice President Chester A. Arthur retreated to his home during the 79 days that President James Garfield fought for his life. He went into self-imposed seclusion in order to dispel any association with the violence that had engulfed the president's life, and he had good reason to do so. Upon shooting two bullets into President Garfield, his assassin shouted, "I did it. I am a Stalwart and Arthur is now president of the United States." From jail, Charles Guiteau had written Arthur, stating that "My inspiration is a godsend to you. It raised you from a political cypher to president of the United States." Rumors had circulated immediately after the attack that the Stalwarts had manufactured the assassination as payback for Garfield's war on corruption. When Secretary of State James Blaine suggested to the vice president that he become acting president during Garfield's illness, Arthur flatly refused and stayed away from Washington, D.C.

Arthur had been nominated in 1880 as Garfield's vice president to appease the Stalwart faction of the Republican Party. A puppet of the corrupt New York Sen. Roscoe Conkling, Arthur had served as the notorious Collector of the Port of New York during most of the 1870s, where he rewarded loyal party workers with jobs in the Customs House. Funds collected from tariffs were funneled to the Republican Party instead of the federal treasury, resulting in Arthur's termination by President Rutherford B. Hayes in 1878 on charges of fraud. When President Garfield finally succumbed to his wounds and died in September 1881, most Americans were expecting a return to corruption in their government. One reformer observed that the new president's past was a "mess of filth." Arthur himself, upon being informed of his predecessor's death, was found face down on his kitchen table, sobbing uncontrollably at the thought of being the new president.

Ex-Senator Conkling and former President Ulysses Grant wasted no time in pressuring President Arthur to appoint Stalwarts to government offices, fully expecting his cooperation based on past allegiances. To everyone's surprise, the president refused to be influenced by Stalwart leaders, declaring, "For the vice presidency, I am indebted to Mr. Conkling. But for the presidency of the United States my debt is to the Almighty." He had been deeply impacted by President Garfield's assassination and immediately began distancing himself from the corruption that had defined his career to this point. He resolved that Garfield's death would not be in vain and felt humbled by the awesome powers of the office to which he had inherited.

At once, he vigorously prosecuted the Star Route Frauds, a kickback scheme involving top-level cronies of the new president's within the Republican Party. He then vetoed one of the largest pork barrel spending projects ever to be approved by Congress, the Rivers and Harbors Bill, and warned Capitol Hill not to send him any further wasteful spending bills. He pressed for post office reform, and cleaned out virtually all corruption by the time he left office. To everyone's surprise, President Arthur chastised Congress after a major government reform plan was rejected in 1882, and pushed hard for its passage in the next session. With the president's backing, the public clamored for reform and Congress passed the sweeping Pendleton Act of 1883. This act established the Civil Service Commission, placing 14,000 government jobs under a merit system. By the beginning of the 20th century, a majority of government jobs were then appointed on merit, ending decades of corruption.

Though entrenched in the filth of fraud and corrupt politics, President Arthur was significantly transformed by the senseless murder of President Garfield for the very reasons he had long championed. Arthur did not lead by charisma or seek to revolutionize how the nation conducted its business, but he did conduct the office with dignity and reverence. He became so ashamed of his past, he instructed that all his official papers be burned. Not surprisingly, the Stalwarts rigged the Republican Party convention so as to replace Arthur with a new candidate in the next election as retribution for his reforms. As one historian has observed, "Arthur's qualities and actions may have been precisely the soothing and conciliatory tonic his ailing country needed at that moment."

※ ※ ※

Case 16 Reflection

1. President Arthur, for all intents and purposes, should have been a corrupt national leader. Yet, he exhibited reverence for the presidency and afforded it the dignity it deserved. Assess how a position of authority can change the mindset of a leader, despite previous transgressions?

2. Many leaders do not exhibit signs of strength until they are tested. What are some examples of leaders who faced adversity and rose to the challenge unexpectedly?

3. Reflect on the significance of President Arthur's championship of civil service reform. How did his support for the Pendleton Act eventually persuade Congress to pass this bill into law?

4. After the assassination of Garfield, President Arthur provided the nation with stability. Why is it important for leaders to provide calm following a jolting event?

5. A dignified and ethical leader does not always succeed if the political winds are blowing a different way, as President Arthur discovered when his party abandoned him during the election of 1884. What costs are associated with leaders who are built on a foundation of ethics and how can this be countered in the political arena?

✳ ✳ ✳

CASE 17: FIGHTING THE STATUS QUO

Theodore Roosevelt (1901-09)

In 1900, Republican Party leaders had orchestrated Theodore Roosevelt's addition to the national ticket as the vice presidential candidate along with incumbent President William McKinley. Most party officials were glad to get rid of Roosevelt from his position as governor of New York and felt he would fade into the woodwork as vice president, a largely ceremonial post at that time. Scarcely six months into his new tenure, though, President McKinley was gunned down by an anarchist, propelling Roosevelt, or "TR", into the president's chair. Senator Mark Hanna, who disliked TR immensely due to his reforms in New York, exclaimed "Now that damn cowboy is in the White House!" Hanna had reason to fear the new president, as Roosevelt believed in a strong executive who could use the office as a "bully pulpit." At the age of 42, the youngest president in American history, TR observed that "There inheres in the presidency more power than in any other office in any great republic...I believe in a strong executive. I believe in power."

TR subscribed to the adage, "Speak softly and carry a big

stick; you will go far" and used this motto to drive reform. He started by ordering the Justice Department to file suit against Northern Securities, a trust with a monopoly on the railroad business. J.P. Morgan, its president, controlled rail lines from Chicago to California and had forced a merger of three railroad companies in 1901, just after TR took office. The president's interference in business matters was unprecedented at that time, and J.P. Morgan paid TR a visit to cut a deal. The president, however, refused to compromise, telling Morgan "That can't be done." The Supreme Court later sided with TR and the trust was permanently broken.

In 1902, the president was faced with a staggering coal strike that brought the nation to its knees for months. Harsh working conditions forced 147,000 coal miners off the job, including many children, at a time before child labor laws and government regulations of the industry. Nearly 500 miners died each year on the job in the United States at that time. The strike produced "untold misery" on the nation as long lines of people waited for small scraps of coal to heat their homes, schools were closed, and hospitals shuttered. TR knew that no president had ever interfered in a strike before, but he felt a moral responsibility to bring the two opposing sides together to end the strike for the sake of the nation.

The representative of the coal mining company refused to negotiate an end to the strike even after President Roosevelt persuaded him of the importance of a settlement. As a result, TR threatened to seize the mines through federal authority and run them himself. A congressman questioned TR's legal authority to do so. The president answered, "The Constitution was made for the people and not the people for the Constitution. I am President of the United States. I am commander in chief of the army. I will give the people coal!" Almost immediately, an arbitration commission set up by TR resolved the stalemate and the strike was over.

In the early 1900s, consumers had no legally sanctioned protections as they do today. President Roosevelt became aware of abuses in the meat packing industry that had led to outbreaks of sickness from food-borne illnesses. After sending a private investigator into various meat packing factories, the president's worst fears were confirmed. At once, he applied pressure to Congress to pass the Meat Inspection Act, giving authority to the Department of Agriculture to inspect meat products shipped across state lines. He then forced Congress to adopt the Pure Food and Drug Act, requiring all food and drug products to have labels affixed to them, advancing the first consumer protection acts in U.S. history.

Another area that the president set his attention to was conservation. He was alarmed by the timber industry's flagrant disregard for forest land and its quickening pace of deforestation. Declaring that "Conservation is a great moral issue," the president placed 150 million acres of timberlands under protective status, the most ever set aside by any American president. He then sought to create five national parks and 18 national monuments, including the Grand Canyon, during his seven-year tenure, almost all over the objections of Congress. TR argued his case for conservation with the people, asserting "We are not building this country of ours for a day. It is to last through the ages." Such were his efforts in this area that his refusal to shoot a wild bear on a hunting trip became the stuff of legends, popularizing "Teddy bears" that have lasted to the present day.

Though largely unsuccessful, President Roosevelt did make attempts to soften prevailing attitudes toward segregation that stubbornly persisted in post-Civil War America. Inviting the noted black educator Booker T. Washington to dinner at the White House, TR became the first president to dine with a member of another race while in office. The event caused a furor among white southerners, with one Memphis newspaper describing it as "the most damnable outrage ever perpetrated by any citizen of the United States." Angrily, TR shot back at those who had criticized him, declaring, "I will choose my own company." Though he was unable to make substantive inroads during his presidency in the area of race relations, this event marked the beginning of a long national debate on equality and fairness for all citizens. The president had taken a first step toward challenging the status quo by fighting the outdated and damaging beliefs and practices that defined his times.

❉ ❉ ❉

Case 17 Reflection

1. President Roosevelt considered the presidency to be a "bully pulpit" by which to highlight important issues. How can leaders learn from this example?

2. TR was an energetic leader who displayed a true enjoyment for the presidency's many challenges. How can a leader's outward attitude impact and influence the organization to which they lead?

3. During the coal strike, President Roosevelt angrily reminded his audience of his authority as president of the United States. When is it appropriate-and when is it not-for leaders to "pull rank" and assert their positional power?

4. Apply TR's signature motto, "Speak softly and carry a big stick" to organizational leadership.

5. President Roosevelt was well ahead of many of his contemporaries in areas such as consumer health, the environment, and race relations. How did he channel this vision into practical application? How can organizational leaders do the same?

6. President Roosevelt did not accept the status quo. What moral responsibility do leaders have to improve the condition of all those in their care?

Google/Public Domain

President Theodore Roosevelt with Educator Booker T. Washington at the White House, October 1901

✱ ✱ ✱

CASE 18: EYEBALL TO EYEBALL

John F. Kennedy (1961-63)

During the late summer of 1962, President John F. Kennedy learned that the Soviet Union was building up offensive missiles in Cuba, just 90 miles off the coast of Florida. The president believed that missiles this close to the U.S. could threaten the military security of the nation, so he warned Soviet leader Nikita Khrushchev to reconsider his country's relationship with Cuba. Khrushchev, in turn, denied that the Soviets were involved in transporting and building missile systems, further warning JFK that a second invasion of Cuba could result in war. On October 14, a U-2 reconnaissance plane took photos clearly indicating that the Soviets were, in fact, installing offensive missile systems in Cuba, contrary to previous assertions by the Kremlin.

President Kennedy immediately convened his top civilian and military advisors to review potential responses to the missile crisis. His advisors provided four options for him to pursue: political pressure followed by a military strike on Cuba; a military strike on Cuba without warning; a naval blockade of incoming Soviet ships to Cuba; and a full-scale invasion of Cuba to remove that nation's leader, Fidel Castro. In the meantime, JFK met with Soviet Foreign Minister Andrei Gromyko, who lied to him regarding the presence of missiles. For the next five days, JFK was advised by most of his top aides to order a bombing of Cuba, though the president was not convinced this was the wisest course of action. Before alerting the American people of the crisis, Kennedy cabled the Soviet leader demanding again that the missiles be removed, with no response.

JFK went on national television to announce the "unmistakable evidence" that offensive missiles were being secretly built in Cuba and to explain his decision to order a naval blockade of the coast of Cuba to stop incoming Soviet ships. As he spoke, air force jets had been dispatched over Florida to protect the United States from a potential Soviet missile launch from Cuba. Historians have since observed that JFK's words during that speech were among the most chilling ever uttered by an American president: "It shall be the policy of this nation to regard any nuclear missile launched from Cuba against any nation in the Western Hemisphere as an attack by the Soviet Union on the United States, requiring a full retaliatory strike upon the Soviet Union.

On October 24, the blockade went into effect as three cruisers, sixteen destroyers, and 150 other ships were dispatched along the island nation's coast. Six Soviet ships were stopped or turned back, causing Secretary of State Dean Rusk to observe, "We're eyeball to eyeball and I think the other fella just blinked." JFK secretly cabled Khrushchev, imploring him to compromise in order to avoid war. The Soviet premier privately cabled Kennedy back, indicating that he was prepared to remove all missiles from Cuba in exchange for a pledge by the U.S. to not invade the island nation again. Kennedy's hope that a deal could be reached was dashed the next day when Khrushchev released a public statement demanding that the U.S. remove all offensive missiles from Turkey in exchange for Soviet concessions. JFK refused, knowing it would severely impact all Western Allies and their collective security.

President Kennedy now faced mounting pressure to resolve the spiralling crisis in order to avoid a potentially catastrophic nuclear showdown. In the end, the president wisely decided to ignore Khrushchev's public deal, instead responding to the private cable that did not include US missile removal from Turkey. However, President Kennedy promised the premier that he would begin phasing out missiles in Turkey as long as the Soviet Union kept this commitment private. Khrushchev agreed, and what became known as the Cuban Missile Crisis came to an end. Immediately following the crisis, both leaders agreed to activate a private cable line with the intent of improving direct communication between the White House and Kremlin. A year later, both nations reached an historic agreement with the signing of the Nuclear Test Ban Treaty, prohibiting further nuclear weapons testing.

※ ※ ※

Case 18 Reflection

1. President Kennedy was advised by most of his military officials to bomb Cuba. Why did he ignore their advice?

2. President Truman once said, "The buck stops here." How did this ring true in this case?

3. Who is ultimately responsible for all decisions made in an organization? Why?

4. Historians regard President Kennedy's handling of the Cuban Missile Crisis as exemplary. What attributes did he employ during this event?

5. How do leaders determine the advice they will follow and the advice they will not?

6. What are some ways that leaders can receive input and advice without committing to following that advice?

7. JFK publicly used strong words to meet the crisis, but explored a more diplomatic course behind the scenes. How did this dual strategy help resolve this case?

8. Provide an example of how a leader can be tough in public, yet flexible enough behind closed doors to seek realistic solutions to pressing problems?

* * *

CASE 19: COMPASSION FOR THE BROKEN

Abraham Lincoln (1861-65)

Though he presided over the most gruesome and grisly war in American history with a human toll worse than all other national wars combined, and considering that he was the civilian head of an army that was determined to hold the Union together at all costs, President Abraham Lincoln found within himself a deep compassion for the broken and downtrodden. Unable at times to endure the heavy burdens of power, the president found himself awake at all hours of the night, worrying about the countless soldiers and civilians who had, and would, die in the conflict.

He regularly sought to visit and comfort wounded soldiers at military hospitals and one day came across a mortally wounded 16-year-old Vermont boy who was serving in the Union army. The president asked, "Well, my poor boy, what can I do for you?" The boy responded that he needed someone to compose a letter to his mother. President Lincoln agreed and sat down to write the letter, promising to send it right away. Then he asked the boy soldier if there was anything he could do for him, and the boy asked: "Won't you stay with me? I do want to hold on to your hand." The president agreed, and for the next two hours sat and comforted the soldier until he died. Folding the boy's hands over his chest, President Lincoln burst out crying at the boy's death and abruptly left the hospital.

Though there have been questions about the authenticity of a letter written by the president to a widow during the fall of 1864, the details of this case do not negate the fact that Lincoln regularly comforted the grieving. Massachusetts Gov. John Andrew asked the president to send his condolences to Mrs. Lydia Bixby upon learning that she had possibly lost five sons in the war. President Lincoln thus wrote these words to the heartbroken mother: "I feel how weak and fruitless must be any word of mine which should attempt to beguile you from the grief of a loss so overwhelming. But I cannot refrain from tendering to you the consolation that may be found in the thanks of the Republic they died to save. I pray that our Heavenly Father may assuage the anguish of your bereavement, and the solemn pride that must be yours, to have laid so costly a sacrifice upon the altar of freedom." Some accounts contend that the president was so overcome with pain for this mother that he personally delivered the letter to her.

Perhaps the greatest example of Abraham Lincoln's extraordinary ability to console and inspire a nation was his address at Gettysburg, Pennsylvania in November 1863, following the bloodiest battle of the war there. Lincoln ran back into the White House to grab a pad of paper before boarding a train for Pennsylvania, with the intention of writing his speech in preparation for the Gettysburg ceremony. On the train, though, the president was approached repeatedly by ordinary citizens seeking his advice and comfort. One grieving father whose son had died in battle sought Lincoln out, with this response from the president: "When I think of the sacrifices of life yet to be offered and the hearts and homes yet to be made desolate before this dreadful war, so wickedly forced upon us, is over, my heart is like a lead within me, and I feel, at times, like hiding in deep darkness."

When President Lincoln's train arrived in Gettysburg, a silent crowd greeted him. Journalist John Forney admonished the gathered people, shaming them, "You gave no cheers to your president. Do you know what you owe to that great man? You owe your country; you owe your name as American citizens." Lincoln worked throughout that night and into the next morning composing the words that would become famous for all time. Awkwardly standing before a crowd of thousands just after a two-hour speech by the famed orator Edward Everett, Abraham Lincoln delivered a two-minute, eloquent, and stirring speech that caused many African Americans standing off to the side to begin weeping loudly, calling out "Amen" repeatedly.

As he paused during the brief speech, some accounts record that the president himself began to weep, wiping his face with a handkerchief before resuming. When the speech had concluded, the hushed audience sat in stunned silence. Many heads were bowed and others had their mouths open as if in disbelief. It took several moments before some audience members began clapping softly. The president quickly took his seat and surmised that the speech had been a failure, unworthy of the occasion. "I should have prepared it with more care," he confided to an aide. It was only later that his words began to be felt by a nation in need of comforting. Historian Douglas Wilson observed that Lincoln's words were a "moving tribute incorporated into an alluring affirmation of the nation's ideals." British lord George Curzon concluded that "it went straight at a declaration of the purpose which animated the soul of Abraham Lincoln, and for which the men buried at Gettysburg had given their lives."

※ ※ ※

JEFFREY J. PORTER

Matthew Brady/Wikimedia

President Abraham Lincoln understood the deep suffering
of his countrymen during the Civil War

Case 19 Reflection

1. Why is it important for leaders to demonstrate a genuine compassion for those whom they lead and serve?

2. Reflect on the adage, "Tough on issues, soft on people."

3. President Lincoln continued his steadfast advocacy for the preservation of the Union while expressing deep emotion at the suffering and casualties around him. How was he able to reconcile these two opposing emotions?

4. Lincoln had a gift for words and the power they can hold. Despite this, he was convinced that his Gettysburg Address was a failure. Why is it sometimes difficult for leaders to gauge the impact of their words on others?

5. President Lincoln's letter to Mrs. Bixby is a model of compassion. How can the president's response serve as a guide for leaders as they seek to comfort the grieving?

6. Leaders at all levels must be sensitive to the struggles of those they lead. How can leaders exhibit compassion?

7. Leadership requires expertise in the area of human resources. How can Lincoln's handling of human suffering provide examples with regards to human resources?

✲ ✲ ✲

CASE 20: REASSURING A STRICKEN NATION

Lyndon B. Johnson (1963-69)

Vice President Lyndon B. Johnson lay face down on the floor with a Secret Service agent on top of him as his limousine sped through the streets of Dallas, Texas, on November 22, 1963 just after 12:30 p.m. He knew something very wrong had occurred in the motorcade to which he had been riding three cars behind his boss, President John F. Kennedy, and these fears were confirmed as agents surrounded him upon arrival at Parkland Hospital. He was rushed to a small windowless room as agents with high-powered rifles stood outside. Johnson was told next to nothing for the next forty minutes while President Kennedy lay dying in a trauma room across the hall. The Secret Service later would admit, "He did not know what we knew- that Kennedy was dead." What the world would soon know is that the single most brutal and dramatic presidential succession in history had just taken place.

Finally, at 1:10 pm, LBJ was advised to leave Dallas and return to Washington, D.C. for security purposes. He refused, concluding that "it would be unthinkable for me to leave with President Kennedy's life hanging in the balance...this is my President and leader...my confidant and friend." At 1:20, he left the hospital in order to wait for Mrs. Kennedy and the casket of the fallen president aboard Air Force One at the airport. Again the Secret Service pleaded with Johnson for an immediate departure, as there had been numerous rumors of a massive plot to take down the entire United States government. Some early media reports indicated that the vice president had been killed along with the president, while others reported that LBJ had suffered a massive heart attack during the ensuing chaos. Though he later reflected that "I think the first thought I had was that this is a terrifying thing that may have international consequences," LBJ again insisted on waiting for Mrs. Kennedy before departing for Washington.

On the ride to the airport, LBJ realized "I could not allow the tide of grief to overwhelm me. The consequences of all my actions were too great for me to become immobilized with emotion. I was a man in trouble, in a world that is never more than minutes away from catastrophe." During this time, he decided to take the oath of office aboard the plane before takeoff in order to reassure the nation that a functioning government was in place despite the assassination. A local judge was summons to the plane to administer the oath and President Johnson allowed one still photo to be released as a symbol of leadership continuity. LIFE Magazine wrote: "In the confusion that followed the assassination, the photograph told the world that there was a new president, and the country that it was safe."

Upon arrival in Washington, President Johnson gave a short speech within full glare of the media in order to further assure the nation that its government had survived. LIFE Magazine wrote that "his eloquence at that moment, so simple as to be stately, defined both a nation's grief and its purpose." Though his helicopter touched down on the South Lawn of the White House, he repeatedly refused the Secret Service's pleas to move into the Executive Mansion. Walking past the West Wing, LBJ averted his eyes out of deference to President Kennedy, ordering the Secret Service to secure the vice presidential residence for his arrival. He would wait several weeks before moving into the White House's private quarters out of respect for the Kennedy family.

President Johnson immediately set out to transpire the business of government, first calling former presidents Truman and Eisenhower to the White House for private counsel and advice. He then called J. Edgar Hoover, head of the FBI, to discuss the progress of an investigation into the assassination. Later that evening, the new president met with bipartisan leaders of Congress, asking for their support and help. The next morning, LBJ moved into the Oval Office and allowed himself to be photographed there, knowing that the American people were in desperate need of symbolic reassurance that the nation was safe. He met with Kennedy's Cabinet and asked them to continue in their posts. Five days after the assassination, President Johnson addressed a joint session of Congress, asking them to pay tribute to JFK's legacy by passing his civil rights bill, which had stalled for months. He pleaded with Congress to "honor the President's memory and continue his work."

The Wall Street Journal summed up the manner to which President Johnson transitioned to the presidency, citing that he "has done much to command respect and encourage confidence."

What is remarkable, though, is that LBJ's "masterpiece of coolheaded improvisation" in the hours following the tragic events in Dallas did not reveal the private thoughts and emotions he wrestled with that day. A declassified transcript from 1978 describes a momentary private encounter where two aides found the new president hiding in a bathroom aboard Air Force One. President Johnson, according to the witnesses, was hysterical with emotion, sobbing, "They're going to kill us all. It's a plot. They killed my president and they're going to kill me."

❊ ❊ ❊

Case 20 Reflection

1. Lyndon B. Johnson succeeded to the nation's highest office under the most brutal, tragic, and public circumstances ever faced by an American president. What important leadership principles did he employ when responding to this crisis?

2. There was a period of immense confusion and misinformation between the time JFK was killed and Lyndon Johnson was sworn in. What can leaders learn from the mistakes made in this case regarding crisis planning?

3. Contrary to popular speculation, this case reinforces President Johnson's loyalty to John F. Kennedy, his boss for three years. Why is it critical that the two top leaders of an organization are loyal to each other?

4. Declassified versions of LBJ's breakdown in an *Air Force One* bathroom illustrate the human side of the new president, though he took great pains to shield these emotions from the public and the press. Why should leaders keep their emotions in check during the performance of their official duties?

5. President Johnson understood the importance of symbolism as he transferred to the presidency. He utilized the presidential airplane, Oval Office, press, and other trappings of office to portray continuity of government operations. What are some ways that leaders use symbolism to enhance their leadership efforts?

6. Leadership transitions can be unsettling and awkward for virtually everyone involved. How can leaders create a smooth transfer of authority on both ends of a change in administration?

IT'S 2AM AT 1600 PENNSYLVANIA AVENUE

Houston Chronicle

Lyndon B. Johnson (right) and Texas Gov. John Connally (center) with JFK hours before the assassination, November 22, 1963

* * *

CASE 21: BATTLING THE SUBORDINATE

James K. Polk (1845-49)

President James K. Polk chose several loyal and competent Cabinet officers to help him govern when he took office in March 1845. Polk's mentor, former President Andrew Jackson, advised Polk to "keep from your cabinet all aspirants to the presidency." Despite this warning, the new president chose the distinguished but ambitious politician James Buchanan to be his secretary of state. Rarely in history has a president and his secretary of state quarreled more than in the case of these two strong-willed men.

The issue of confronting Great Britain for the territory of Oregon proved contentious at Cabinet meetings in the fall of 1845. The secretary of state sought to be cautious with Britain, imploring President Polk to wait on the Oregon dispute until relations with Mexico were evident. Polk shot back, "We should do our duty towards both Mexico and Great Britain and firmly maintain our rights and leave the rest to God and country." Buchanan insisted that the president's stance would mean war on both the northern and southern boundaries of the United States, stating that "your greatest danger is that you will be attacked for having a warlike tone." President Polk responded, "My greatest danger is that I would be attacked for having yielded to what was done by my predecessors."

The president knew that his secretary of state was secretly discussing the Oregon strategy with former secretary of state John C. Calhoun, one of Polk's rivals. Polk chose to ignore this certainty at the time, but became frustrated when he later reached a settlement with Great Britain. Asking for his Cabinet's recommendation on whether to send the treaty to the Senate, all favored the settlement except for Buchanan, who had reversed himself and was willing to wage war for additional land. Buchanan accused his boss of "backing out on the true friends of the administration" and at first refused to assist in drafting or supporting the treaty's contents. The secretary even hinted that he may draft his own version of the treaty without the president's consent and submit it to the Senate independently. President Polk confronted him, asking "Do you wish to draw up a paper of your own in order to make an issue with me?" Buchanan responded that his boss's remark "struck him through the heart," but he fell into line and pledged to support Polk's version of the treaty after being given an "unpleasant" ultimatum to do so.

In May 1846, the United States was on the eve of war with Mexico. Secretary of State Buchanan told the Cabinet that a condition of the war should be to leave California alone for fear of angering Great Britain and France and inciting a potential war with both countries. President Polk and Buchanan argued bitterly over the issue for a length of time in front of the Cabinet officers until the president exploded, "Before I would make a pledge like that I would meet the war with England or France or all the powers of

Christendom and that I would stand and fight until the last man." Polk vowed to take California by force if he desired and to wage war on any nation who tried to stop him.

For a period of time after this confrontation, the secretary of state considered resigning. Instead, he asked Polk for an appointment to the Supreme Court, which had a vacancy. The president refused to appoint him, and Buchanan reluctantly decided to stay in the Cabinet. Hoping to persuade President Polk to appoint Buchanan's close political ally to the Court, the secretary met privately with his boss to convince him of the wisdom of such an appointment. The president provided the secretary of state with some vague assurances, enough so that Buchanan circulated the news to the prospective nominee and powerful political allies. Polk, though, went on to nominate one of Buchanan's political rivals without first alerting the secretary of state of his decision. Buchanan angrily went to the White House to confront his boss, only to be rebuffed, "As President I am responsible for my appointments...I have a perfect right to make them without consulting with my Cabinet." The nomination failed in the Senate and President Polk suspected his secretary of state's involvement in sabotaging the appointment.

Later, after Zachary Taylor was elected president in November 1848, Buchanan asked Polk's permission to visit with Taylor. Polk refused, saying no present administration official should solicit the incoming president. Buchanan stormed out of the president's office in disgust. Polk wrote in his diary that day that he considered his secretary of state to be "an able man, but sometimes he acts like an old maid." There has been much speculation as to why President Polk chose to retain his secretary of state and why Buchanan chose to stay on throughout Polk's term. The historian Charles McCoy observed that "President Polk was able and willing to keep Buchanan in his Cabinet, for he could never dominate the President."

❉ ❉ ❉

President and Mrs. Polk (center), Secretary of State Buchanan (left) with Dolley Madison (right), outside the White House before a reception, February 1849

Case 21 Reflection

1. Why do you think President Polk decided to keep Secretary of State Buchanan in his Cabinet throughout his term? What were his real motives for doing so?

2. What are the benefits and drawbacks that come from retaining a staff member who is challenging to manage?

3. President Polk knew that Buchanan was scheming behind his back regarding the Oregon boundary dispute. Why did the president not confront him at that time? How can it be beneficial for leaders to learn information about their subordinates, yet withhold discipline?

4. President Polk finally confronted Buchanan when he threatened to draft his own treaty with Great Britain in direct opposition to the president's plan. For blatant insubordination, why is it critical for leaders to take immediate action? What risks may result from not doing so?

5. With regards to hiring staff, how should leaders demonstrate a willingness to be collaborative, yet retain the final decision for hiring decisions?

6. President Polk observed that his secretary of state was competent, but difficult to handle. How--and to what extent--should leaders reconcile this conflict?

* * *

CASE 22: FIRM HOLD ON THE ELECTORATE

Franklin D. Roosevelt (1933-45)

Franklin D. Roosevelt was governor of New York in 1932 when he first ran for the presidency in the midst of the Great Depression. Incumbent President Herbert Hoover was hopelessly unpopular for his insistence that government was not the answer to the nation's woes. Roosevelt, or FDR, seized on Hoover's doleful outlook by countering with his theme song, "Happy Days are Here Again" while stating frequently, "I pledge you, I pledge myself, to a new deal for the American people." Knowing that voters wondered about the severity of his polio, FDR became the first candidate to accept his party's nomination in person, hoping to downplay rumors of his illness. Hoover attempted to gain traction against Roosevelt's early and steady lead by actively campaigning, only to experience hostile crowds and apathy towards his ideas. Though the sitting president warned that FDR's election would mean that "grass would grow in the streets of a hundred cities, a thousand towns," hardly anyone was paying attention. On Election Day 1932, FDR took 57% of the popular vote to Hoover's 40%, securing 472 electoral votes to 59. Voters agreed with FDR that "above all, try something" was a better course of action than no action at all.

As 1936 began, Franklin Roosevelt's New Deal programs had become ingrained in the fabric of the national culture and there was a dramatic shift in the relationship between the people and their government. Though the wealthy referred to him as "that man" and a "traitor to his class," FDR was wildly popular with the general public. His only real political threat had been Sen. Huey Long of Louisiana, a radical, who was assassinated before he was able to get into the race. The Republican challenger was Gov. Alfred Landon of Kansas who tried to jumpstart his campaign by claiming he could manage the New Deal better than Roosevelt, its architect. When that did not work, Landon resorted to denouncing New Deal programs such as Social Security, which he described as putting "half of the people of America under federal control."

Landon was no match for the charismatic FDR, losing by a landslide to the president with 37% of the vote compared to Roosevelt's shattering 61%. The Electoral College count was just as damaging with FDR garnering 523 votes to Landon's 8. President Roosevelt also changed the landscape of the voting patterns in the nation for decades to come by appealing to voters in large cities, the middle class, the poor, laborers, and African-Americans. A black leader at that time instructed all African-Americans to "Go home and turn Lincoln's picture to the wall. That debt has been paid in full." One newspaper reflected on the landslide results: "The water of liberalism has been dammed up for 40 years. The dam is out. Landon went down the creek in a torrent."

By 1940, most observers did not expect President Roosevelt to run for a third term, as no president in history had served more than two terms out of respect for George Washington's precedent. FDR did not run in the primaries, nor did any other serious candidate, leaving a void by the time the Democratic convention took place that summer. The president remained silent during the convention until a draft movement began in which he was overwhelmingly re-nominated by his party with the theme "Don't switch horses in the middle of the stream." The Republican Party turned to a dark horse candidate in the person of Wendell L. Willkie, who was described as a "simple, barefoot Wall Street lawyer." Willkie, who likened the president to "The Champ," found himself with very little to criticize and thus resorted to making FDR's potential third term his major emphasis. A popular campaign slogan stated that "Two times is enough for any man," referring to President Roosevelt's two terms in office.

The president stayed out of the campaign circuit until October when polls suggested the race had tightened in Willkie's favor. Willkie warned voters that the developments in Europe regarding war would mean that "If you re-elect him you may expect war in April, 1941." The president refuted his challenger, declaring "I have said this before, but I shall say it again and again: Your boys are not going to be sent into any foreign wars." It worked. FDR was reelected to a third term with 55% of the popular vote and 449 electoral votes to Willkie's 82.

World War II had been raging for almost four years when the 1944 campaign opened. President Roosevelt had been in office nearly 12 years and the cares of office had accelerated his aging process considerably. The once vital president had been reduced to a visibly haggard and frail man. It was during this fourth and final campaign that FDR faced his most competitive challenger, Gov. Thomas Dewey of New York. Dewey went on the attack from the beginning, calling the Roosevelt administration a group of "stubborn men grown old and tired in office." The Republican candidate went on to criticize "one-man government" due to FDR's long tenure in the presidency, but then contradicted himself when suggesting that "Communists are seizing control of the New Deal." FDR cleverly rebutted these accusations, saying "Now, really, which is it? Communism or monarchy? I want neither."

In order to silence his critics and reassure the public that he was not too old and tired for a fourth term, FDR set out on a stringent campaign schedule in October, traveling to major cities to rouse support. One aide commented, "After the people have seen him, they can make up their own minds about his vigor and health." In New York City, he rode in an open car for 51 miles in the pouring rain among the millions of people who lined the streets to see him. Unbeknownst to the people, the president was taken out of the motorcade every few blocks in order to dry him before returning to the streets where he waved and flashed his famous smile. A week before the election, Dewey charged that FDR had sent a destroyer at taxpayer expense to pick up his dog, Fala. President Roosevelt responded in mock outrage and wit, relating that his dog's "Scotch soul was furious. He has not been the same dog since." President Roosevelt won a fourth term with 53% to 46% for Dewey and a margin of 432 to 99 in the Electoral College. Afterwards, the president described his last election as "the meanest campaign of his life." Within a few months, he was dead of a stroke.

IT'S 2AM AT 1600 PENNSYLVANIA AVENUE

* * *

FDR Presidential Library

President Roosevelt's last campaign, New York City, October 1944

Case 22 Reflection

1. President Roosevelt served longer than any president in history. What are some reasons that he maintained such a firm hold on the electorate?

2. FDR remained unusually popular during his twelve years in office, with much of this attributed to his force of personality. How did his responses to challengers during the campaigns provide a glimpse of the president's engaging connection to voters?

3. Longevity in public leadership positions is rare today. Franklin Roosevelt's long tenure was reassuring to many Americans who came to trust him on a personal level. What are some obstacles to the fulfillment of long-term commitments by organizational leaders today?

4. Some leaders who have stayed in one position for a lengthy time accumulate detractors. Weigh the pros and cons of lengthy tenures for organizational leaders.

5. Even 1940 opposition leader Wendell Willkie acknowledged Roosevelt as "The Champ" due to his mysterious pull with the electorate. What can be attributed to both strong and weak connections between leaders and those they serve?

※ ※ ※

TEST YOUR KNOWLEDGE

Match the leadership skill with the American President who most exemplified this skill.

a. Harry S Truman
b. Andrew Jackson
c. Franklin D. Roosevelt
d. John Tyler
e. Woodrow Wilson
f. Dwight Eisenhower
g. James K. Polk
h. Richard M. Nixon
i. Abraham Lincoln
j. John F. Kennedy
k. George W. Bush
l. Ronald Reagan
m. James A. Garfield
n. Chester A. Arthur
o. Theodore Roosevelt
p. Lyndon B. Johnson

_____1. Successful attention to details and direct involvement of executive leadership.

_____2. Strong, confident, and moral leadership used to reassure and provide calm.

_____3. Vibrant, activist leadership approach aimed at forcing needed change.

_____4. Despite powerful and skillful subordinates, the executive reserves and affirms the ultimate power to make and carry out decision-making.

_____5. Attempting to understand and connect with opposing points of view.

_____6. Management of personnel using progressive disciplinary methods.

_____7. Holding firm against political pressures.

_____8. Moral leadership designed to rectify societal ills.

_____9. Ability to motivate and inspire through words, actions, and personal example.

_____10. Honest and moral governance by rejecting a history of corruption.

_____11. Positive and activist leadership approach to solving problems and moving forward.

_____12. Weighing all options available with precision, common sense, and timing.

_____13. Political skill that is built on a legacy of optimism and a can-do attitude regarding the future.

_____14. Perseverance and refusal to give up, without succumbing to negative expectations.

_____15. Using force when persuasion fails and the circumstances require it.

_____16. Competent negotiations grounded in establishing productive working relationships with known adversaries for the purpose of improving existing conditions.

_____17. Public display of stability, calmness, confidence, and strength, even if inner doubts and fears are reality for the leader.

_____18. Visionary leadership enhanced by effective oratorical abilities and moral convictions.

_____19. Connecting with the deep human yearning for compassion and purpose that can change the course of events.

_____20. Wise enforcement of laws and policies that are carried out in a fair and ethical manner.

_____21. Level-headed and pragmatic approach to solving a crisis that directly addresses the same factors leading to the crisis in the first place.

_____22. Honest and moral governance that challenges established tradition and accepted norms that have plagued the organization in the past, even in the wake of powerful opposition.

ANSWER KEY

1. G
2. K
3. O
4. G
5. H
6. A
7. D
8. I
9. C
10. N
11. J
12. I
13. C
14. A
15. F
16. L
17. P
18. E
19. I
20. B
21. J
22. M

✻ ✻ ✻

REFERENCES

Ahlers, M. and Jones, A. "Tape Sheds Light on Surreal Nixon-Protesters Meeting." *CNN*, November 10, 2011.

Beschloss, M. (1991). *The Crisis Years: Kennedy and Khrushchev 1960-63.* New York, NY: HarperCollins Publishers.

Bowman, J. (1998). *The History of the American Presidency.* North Dighton, MA: World Publications Group, Inc.

Brands, H.W. (2003). *Woodrow Wilson.* New York, NY: Henry Holt and Company.

Brown v. Board of Education of Topeka, KS, 347 U.S. 483, May 17, 1954.

Burns, J. (1970). *Roosevelt: The Lion and the Fox.* Old Saybrook, CT: Konecky and Konecky.

Burstein, A. (2003). *The Passions of Andrew Jackson.* New York, NY: Alfred A. Knopf.

Carnahan, B. (2007). *Act of Justice: Lincoln's Emancipation Proclamation and the Law of War.* Lexington, KY: University Press of Kentucky.

Carney, J. and Dickerson, J. "Inside the War Room." *TIME Magazine*, vol. 158, no. 28, (2001): 112-125.

Carnog, E. and Whelan, R. (2000). *Hats in the Ring: An Illustrated History of American Presidential Campaigns.* New York, NY: Random House.

Cooper, J. (2009). *Woodrow Wilson.* New York, NY: Alfred A. Knopf Publishing.

Dallek, R. (2003). *An Unfinished Life: John F. Kennedy.* Boston, MA: Little, Brown, and Company.

Davis, K. (1945). *Dwight D. Eisenhower: Soldier of Democracy.* Old Saybrook, CT: Konecky and Konecky.

Donald, D. (1995). *Lincoln.* New York, NY: Simon and Schuster.

Drury, A. (1971). *Courage and Hesitation: Notes and Photographs of the Nixon Administration.* Garden City, NY: Doubleday and Company, Inc.

Duram, J. (1981). *A Moderate Among Extremists: Dwight D. Eisenhower and the School Desegregation Crisis.* Chicago, IL: Nelson-Hall.

Eisenhower, D. (1957). "Dwight D. Eisenhower's Little Rock Response." www.TeacherVision.com.

Flagel, T. (2007). *The History Buff's Guide to the Presidents.* Naperville, IL: Cumberland House Publishers.

Fraser, C. (2000). "Crossing the Color Line in Little Rock: The Eisenhower Administration and the Dilemma of Race for U.S. Foreign Policy." *Diplomatic History,* vol. 24, no. 2: 233-264.

Freedman, R. (1987). *Lincoln: A Photobiography.* New York, NY: Clarion Books.

Garraty, J. (1983). *The American Nation: A History of the U.S. to 1877,* 5th edition, Vol. 1. New York, NY: Harper and Row Publishers.

Garraty, J. (1991). *The American Nation: A History of the U.S. Since 1865,* 7th edition, New York, NY: Harpers Collins Publishers.

Geis, J. (1971). *Franklin D. Roosevelt: Portrait of a President.* Garden City, NJ: Doubleday and Company, Inc.

Gillon, S. (2009). *The Kennedy Assassination 24 Hours Later: Lyndon B. Johnson's Pivotal First Day as President.* New York, NY: Perseus Books Group.

Gillon, S. (2011)."Facing Down Infamy." *History Magazine,* vol. 9, no. 6: 20-28.

Gould, L. (2003). *The Modern American Presidency.* Lawrence, KS: University Press of Kansas.

Jackson, R. (2003). *That Man: An Insider's Portrait of Franklin D. Roosevelt.* Oxford, UK: Oxford University Press.

Kenney, C. (2000). *John F. Kennedy.* New York, NY: BBS Public Affairs.

Kirk, J. (2007). *Beyond Little Rock: The Origins and Legacies of the Central High Crisis.* Fayetteville, AR: University of Arkansas Press.

Kortenhof, K. (2010). "Battle over Korea: Who's In Charge?" *History Magazine,* vol. 8, no. 3: 32-38.

Kostyal, K. M. (2009). *Abraham Lincoln's Extraordinary Era.* Washington, D.C.: National Geographic Society.

Kraft, B. (2003). *Theodore Roosevelt, Champion of the American Spirit.* New York, NY: Clarion Books.

Krannawitter, T. (2008). *Vindicating Lincoln: Defending the Politics of our Greatest President.* Lanham, MD: Rowman and Littlefield Publishing Company.

Kunhardt, P. (2008). *Looking for Lincoln.* New York, NY: Random House.

Lorant, S. (1968). *The Glorious Burden: The American Presidency.* New York, NY: Harper and Row Publishers.

Manchester, W. (1983). *Remembering Kennedy: One Brief Shining Moment.* Boston, MA: Little, Brown, and Co.

Martin, A. (2007). *Theodore Roosevelt and the Rise of Modern America.* New York, NY: Dutton Books.

Matuz, R. (2004). *The Presidents' Fact Book.* New York, NY: Black Dog and Leventhal Publishers.

McCullough, D. (1992). *Truman.* New York, NY: Simon and Schuster.

McPherson, J. (2000). *To the Best of My Ability.* London, UK: Dorling Kindersley Books.

Meyerowitz, J. (2006). *Aftermath: World Trade Center.* New York, NY: Phaidon Press, Inc.

Morris, E. (1999). *Dutch: A Memoir of Ronald Reagan.* New York, NY: Random House.

Morris, E. (2001). *Theodore Rex.* New York, NY: Random House.

Morris, J. (1996). *The Reagan Way.* Minneapolis, MN: Learner Publications Inc.

O'Brien, C. (2004). *Secret Lives of the U.S. Presidents.* Philadelphia, PA: Quirk Books.

Press Association. (2002). *9-11: A Tribute.* Surrey, UK: TAJ Books.

Ritchie, D. (1999). *American History: The Modern Era Since 1865.* New York, NY: McGraw-Hill.

Rubel, D. (1994). *Encyclopedia of the Presidents and their Times.* New York, NY: Scholastic Books.

Sandburg, C. (1970). *Abraham Lincoln: The Prairie Years and the War Years.* Pleasantville, NY: Reader's Digest.

Sandler, M. (2008). *Lincoln Through the Lens.* New York, NY: Walker and Company.

Seigenthaler, J. (2003). *James K. Polk.* New York, NY: Henry Holt and Company.

Shefchik, R. (2011). "The Reagan Century." *History Magazine*, vol. 9, no. 1: 30-35.

Sidey, H. (2000). *Portraits of the Presidents: Power and Personality in the Oval Office.* New York: Time Books.

Smith, C. (2004). *Presidents: All You Need to Know.* Irvington, NY: Hylas Publishers.

Sorensen, T. (1965). *Kennedy.* New York, NY: Harper and Row Publishers.

St. George, J. (1999). *In the Line of Fire: Presidents' Lives at Stake.* New York, NY: Scholastic, Inc.

TIME Magazine. (1998). *TIME 75 Years 1923-1998.* New York, NY: TIME Books.

TIME Magazine. (2002). *TIME Person of the Year 75th Anniversary edition.* New York, NY: TIME Books.

TIME Magazine. (2001). *American Legends.* New York, NY: TIME Books.

Time-Life Books. (1998). *The American Dream: The 1950s.* Alexandria, VA: Time-Life Books.

Tindall, G. (1984). *America: A Narrative History, Vol. 2.* New York, NY: W.W. Norton and Company.

Trost, C. and Bennett, S. (2003). *President Kennedy Has Been Shot.* Naperville, IL: Sourcebooks, Inc.

Truman, H. (1955). *Memoirs by Harry S. Truman.* Old Saybrook, CT: Konecky and Konecky.

Ventura, S. (2003). *The Leadership Secrets of Santa Claus.* Dallas, TX: Walk the Talk Company.

Wagner, H. (2004). *Ronald Reagan.* Philadelphia, PA: Chelsea House Publishers.

Walsh, K. (2003)."Dark Day: Kennedy Assassination." *U.S. News and World Report*, vol. 135, no. 18: 50-57.

Whitney, D. (1996). *The American Presidents: Biographies of the Chief Executives, 8th Edition.* Pleasantville, NY: Reader's Digest Association, Inc.

Wilentz, S. (2008). *The Age of Reagan: A History 1974-2008.* New York, NY: Harpers Collins Publishers.

Wright, J. (2008). *Campaigning for President.* New York, NY: Harpers Collins Publishers.

Young, D. (2006). *Dear Mr. President: Letters to the Oval Office.* Washington, D.C: National Geographic Society.

❧ ❧ ❧

* * *

ABOUT THE AUTHOR

Jeffrey J. Porter lives in southern Maine, where he was born and raised, and is married with two children. An amateur historian since his 8th grade year, he has studied American presidential history in depth with an interest in the personalities and leadership styles of the White House occupants who have contributed to our nation's history.

Mr. Porter has served as a public school educator since 1993 in a variety of roles, including teacher, school principal, assistant superintendent, and currently superintendent of schools. As a veteran educational leader, he has discovered common connections between organizational leadership and the lessons taught by the nation's chief executives, the basis for this book.

The author holds a bachelor's degree in education with a minor in history from the University of Maine, a master's degree in educational administration from the University of Maine, and a postgraduate degree in educational leadership from the University of Southern Maine. He has recently completed doctoral work in the area of American public policy.

Jeffrey J. Porter

* * *

AFTERWORD

United States presidential history and the actors who have stepped onto the national stage during their anointed time is a history of the American people themselves. From out of the crowd have arisen national leaders for the day, some prepared and others not as much. But still, for the vast majority of the 230 years of the revered institution, even lesser men have risen to the occasion for the cause of democracy. Let us never forget that the United States, like all other States, is dependent upon God. As Job 12:23 relays, "He makes nations rise and then fall, builds up some and abandons others." [MSG] It is only by the grace of the Almighty that the United States shall continue to prosper. God annoints our leaders to do His work, and it is our duty to protect the presidential office as sacred in fulfilling His work on earth.

JEFFREY J. PORTER

Made in the USA
Columbia, SC
04 November 2022

08121579-7d65-4ec2-a13b-a7b59ebc2a13R01